Pyrography for Beginners

A Step by Step Guide to Craft 15 Awesome Wood Burning Art, Patterns and Projects with Essential Woodburning Tips and Tools | Wood Burning Book for Kids and Adults

By

Luke Byrd

Disclaimer

This publication is designed to provide competent and reliable information regarding the subject matter covered. However, the views expressed in this publication are those of the author alone, and should not be taken as expert instruction or professional advice. The reader is responsible for his or her own actions.

The author hereby disclaims any responsibility or liability whatsoever that is incurred from the use or application of the contents of this publication by the purchaser or reader. The purchaser or reader is hereby responsible for his or her own actions.

Table of Contents

Introduction

Have you tried out pyrography before? Or did you probably do it once or twice some time back without any real idea as to how the art goes? Be real now; it is time to study how to use pyrography wood and pen to make something beautiful. Luckily for you, the tools used in this art are cheap and easy to get, at least, compared to the previous ages.

Pyrography, which is generally referred to most times as woodburning, is an art that helps you to make excellent designs on the surface of any wood—basswood, birch, pine, anything! So, at the end of this course, you'll be able to decorate your vases, ornaments, cutleries, boxes, tables, and even make more intricate designs! However, the techniques used here are only compatible with wood and not with any other material like leather or ceramics.

This book will focus deeply on the art of pyrography. It has in-depth guidelines explaining every process involved in wood burning with pictures to engage your mind actively. Besides knowing how to do the craft, you will also be informed of every piece of equipment you might need for each step. So, with the heavy load of information packed in this book, series of practice, and a well of patience, you will gradually become a PRO at pyrography!

Chapter 1

What is Pyrography?

Pyrography is a rich form of art that involves embellishing surfaces like wood by burning intricate designs across them. Burns usually aren't marks that the human eye would appreciate, but then, pyrography brings a whole new definition to the table. Coined from two Latin words, 'pur' which means fire and 'graphos' which means writing, you could deduct that this art indeed involves you writing with fire!

Contrary to the image a layperson would paint in his mind, this art does not involve burning a whole mass of wood until it becomes ash dust! All you need to do is use a heated metallic object to burn through the surface very lightly, forming beautiful engravings in the process.

History of Pyrography

Pyrography is an art that has been in existence for a time even longer than clothes have! The early men adored this art as they used it to show status, skills and emotions. Apart from these, the early men also did not have to use complex tools like colors, brushes or pastels at that time. All they needed for this art was fire and wood. Wood existed everywhere, and that was a big plus for them. Also, when they struck two granite stones against each other, the friction produced fire. It was with that fire they heated metals. All the vigor involved in pyrography at that time made it get closed off as a work for males only.

Pyrography was the first form of artwork to exist in the whole world. So, it was with this art that the early men with artistic skills used to practice drawing. They used the art to draw on their walls, beautiful patterns that are now called the mural painting. The use of fire for artwork can be traced back to the Egyptians, Chinese, Romans and a few Africans. Then, it was called the 'Fire Needle' embroidery. You know, just like you would sew threads through a piece of fabric, the early men saw pyrography as passing streaks of fire through surfaces like wood. Hence, the reason it was termed that ingenious name.

The fire couldn't have just been introduced directly to the wood as it would have led to the whole mass getting burnt. So, the early men heated stones with the fire and used it to mark faint lines on wood. It was only later on that the use of metal for engraving wood was discovered.

The evidence that this art dates far back can be found in South American Pyrography. The South American Nazca mate cup was one wooden piece whose sides were dotted with the engraving of hummingbirds sucking nectar. The engraving was only able to stand the test of time because standard pyrography tools were used.

Back in the days, during the medieval and Victorian eras, marking wood with burns was something ubiquitous and enjoyable. However, the majority of the artworks lost their quality over time since they were made with make-shift tools. The tools used then was a pot whose lid had several holes. Within the pots were heaps of coals that were heated by a stove. The artists would then push pointed rods through the holes and wait for them to get heated before driving the red-hot mouths through wooden surfaces.

The issue with the stove and pot equipment was the fact that on bringing them out of the coal pot, they would lose their heat. And that meant that the carvings could not be done effectively and quickly. This method was termed as the 'Poker wood' technique, the next after the 'Fire needle embroidery'.

However, as time went on, around the 20th century, an architect, Melbourne was able to crack out a piece of better equipment for pyrography. Through his studies, he discovered that the art would get better once the heat of the pokers could be retained. So, to achieve that, he forced hot puffs of benzene through a hot carving pencil. The pencil was formed out of platinum and connected to a jar filled with benzene. The fumes of benzene within the pencil succeeded in keeping it hot, and that meant he could make deeper engravings.

With this simple and less stressful discovery, pyrography took a new turn and women began to try it out. In no time, women were able to change the essence of pyrography into something natural when they started to use it to adorn their homes.

How Does Pyrography Work?

To bring out the beauty of pyrography, you will need a few equipment.

- A pyrography pen.
- A slab of wood with a smooth surface.
- An abrasive like sandpaper.
- A transfer paper made from graphite.
- Scissors.
- A tape.
- A stencil for your burning procedure.

The most receptive surface for pyrography is wood. That is why, in this section, we will be focusing on wood as the material.

The first thing you should do is get your wood ready and inspect the surfaces for dents or scratches. If there are any such things, you may have to smoothen the surfaces with sandpaper until you get an even surface.
If you are sure of the quality of your skills, you can start burning into the wood right away. This way, you can creatively burn out the design in your head with your free-hand. However, if you feel you might make a

mistake using your free hand, stick to using a stencil. With this, you can achieve higher levels of precision.

To use a stencil:
1. Use your scissors to rip through your graphite paper until it has the same dimensions as the wood.
2. Align the image you want to burn into the wood on the graphite paper and then, use the tape to hold them against each other.
3. Ensure that the side to be transferred is made to face the graphite paper.

Trace the image with the pen you prepared, making sure to highlight every curve you want to see on the wood. When you are done, take away the graphite paper.

Now that you have traced out the image on the wood surface, you have to burn through the tracings next. Burning is done with a pyrography pen. They work similarly to the iron used to solder materials together. The pen has a tip made of brass that gets heated by the flow of electric current.

As you burn through the wood, ensure that you remove the tip of the pen from the wood at intervals. The longer the contact the pen has with the wood, the more intense the burn gets. So, in cases where you want to see effects similar to that of pencil shading, you can leave the tip of the pen on the surface for a longer time.

There is a pen tip suitable for all burning purposes, and this is what you should get as a beginner. With it, you can burn through straight lines and design outlines quickly. The pens with solid tips help to burn out big lines that require a lot of emphases.

Generally, the degree at which you press the pen to the wooden surface will help you get several tones, all ranging between the lightest shades of brown to the deepest shades.

Benefits of Pyrography

- Pyrography can be a great way of achieving communication. This particular benefit played out well in the medieval ages as there were no phones, fax machines or sheets of paper and ink to use in communicating. So, instead, they used fire to write on walls, and it lasted pretty much for some time. So, anyone who saw the writings would usually get informed of something important.

- Pyrography helps to instil in people a rare sense of confidence and ownership. How would you feel on seeing your work hung up on the walls of your best friend's room? Indeed, seeing the intricate designs will only make you feel excited. Also, in the olden days, beautiful curves and designs were engraved on the kitchenware of the royals. So, that way, they were quickly recognized.

- The art of pyrography can help you reduce boredom and also make you some cool money! Back in the Victorian age, the welders and local crafters used this art to make money. They would carve out beautiful designs on gourds, wooden boards, furniture and even cutlery with fire and sell those items to people.

- It can be used as aesthetical purposes. Having a wood-engraved with burn marks to form the image of a lion is bound to draw some attention from people. That is why many museums and art galleries out there are bent on gathering materials affected by the pyrography process. You could also use such materials to reduce the severity of the walls in your room.

- Pyrography is an art that does not operate on too many expenses. All you need to do is get a pyrography pen and a suitable material for the procedure, at the very least. All of these are things you can get at pretty affordable prices.

Chapter 2

Wood Burning Tips, Tricks, and Techniques

Wood burning is a fascinating branch of pyrography that dwells deeply on inscribing burn marks across the wood's surface. However, it is also a very intricate work of art that requires a high degree of meticulousness, patience, steadiness, and so much more – and in this section, we will take a look at what they are, which are termed as tips, tricks, and techniques! First, they work to spray your work with a vital air of professionalism that will get people awe-stricken. Knowing useful tricks when it comes to wood burning will also save you a lot of stress, money, and time. So, let's delve into them and work on making a professional out of you!

Tricks for Wood Burning Tools

Like how a baker would have a secret ingredient she adds to her pastries, designers involved in wood burning also need to have some personal tools that get the job done. First, let's acquaint ourselves with the preliminary tools. They include the following:

1.   A pyrography pen.

2.   A myriad of tips for the pyrography pen.

3.   Wood slabs.

4.   Sandpaper or any abrasive compound like oxides of Aluminum.

5.   A grip for the pyrography pen (a clay pot).

Now that we know what the tools are, the next thing to do is study each one and see how we can get maximum efficiency.

The pyrography pen

This pen is structured just like the common pen we use for writing. The only difference that exists is that the pyrography pen works electrically and releases fumes in the process. It is this fume that burns through the wood.

All you have to do is plug in the pen's switch to a socket with stable electricity, and leave it to rest against its grip for about five minutes for it to get hot. Once the tip has attained the right temperature, press it against the wood, and burn out your designs.

The above procedure sounds pretty simple, but then many necessary precautions and steps are missing. Let's discover them.

- Before you plug in your pen to the socket, make sure you must have inserted the tip you will be using for the burning to its mouth. Once the mouth gets hot, it takes a pretty long time to cool back down, and that could pose a big problem when it comes to changing the tip.

- If you have to change the tip of an already hot pyrography pen, make sure you do not try using your bare hands! A pair of pliers with a firm grip will suffice instead.

- In case you have to suddenly stop using the pen while burning, make sure you do not leave it lying carelessly on your work table. Allow it to lie against its grip. It will save you from having scalds and burns inflicted on your skin.

- When you are not using your pyrography pen, unplug it from the socket!

- Before using your pen on your final wood piece, make sure you try it out on some sample material to get yourself accustomed to its heat and pressure settings. It would help if you also studied the time it takes for the pen to make light burns and deep burns.

- When burning the outlines of your design, do not press the pen to the lines! Pressing too hard can cause black burns that may not be easy to get rid of from the slab. So, try to move as fluidly and softly as possible, making light burns at first. If you need to darken anything later, you can move your pen over the light burns again. It is much safer that way.

- Start your burning procedure from light traces to darker ones. Outlines with heavy shades of black cannot be corrected as quickly as the light shades can. Be careful.

- Follow the grain of the wood you use while burning. You can identify the graining pattern of a slab of wood by tracing the lines that taper from one end to the other. So, when using your pen, direct the tip along the direction of those grain lines. Doing anything, on the contrary, will only oppose the swift move of the pen's nib.

- Make sure you align the outline of the picture you want to use on the wood in such a way that it faces you. So when you drive your pen along the edges, your hands move towards you.

- Burn the outlines of your design before heading over to the complex interior arcs and curves. Start lightly at first before furthering into something deeper and darker.

- Solid pyrography pen nibs are used for burning bold and dark outlines. Please do not make the mistake of using it where you ought to have used a pen with a looped nib. Looped nibs are meant for the light shading of your designs. When you get your new pyrography pen, you will get about four to seven different tips. Make sure you know the use of each one before using them to avoid making mistakes.

- As you use your pen, ensure you use something to clean the tip. The mouth is usually stained with carbon soot due to the fumes. So, clean the tips to ensure an even shade of burn throughout the outlines. For this, you can get a wet towel, which you can use to clean the tips regularly. A tea strainer would also do the trick! Run the tip of your pen across the lower mash and watch the soot fall off neatly. Failure to do this could tamper with the pen's heat regulatory system, making it hard to work with the device.

- If you notice too much soot from the pyrography pen, it could mean the tips are already too hot. To solve this, pull out the pen's plug from the socket and allow the temperature to reduce to a much lower value.

Wood slabs

The wood is an essential material needed for this artwork. It bears the designs and the burns. If the wood has problems, it means the whole work is a waste. So, to prevent such from happening, below are a few tips and tricks you should be aware of:

- What kind of wood are you using? There are two types of wood. There are the hardwood and the softwood. The softwood doesn't oppose burning as much as hardwood, and they are great for beginners! You'd even be surprised at how cheap they are. Softwood also has pale colorations that make your burned outlines stand out proudly. Examples of softwood include basswood, pine, and so on.

- There are also a few wood types we would discuss here. And then, there are a few tricks that might help you get the best from them.

1. The Italian poplar plywood: This wood has a light coloration that makes burn marks come out prominently and beautifully. It also has an even graining system that makes burning much more comfortable. However, when using your pyrography pencil on the surface of this wood, make sure you make very light burns. Deep burns will mean you are eating deep into the glue that holds the pieces together.
2. Maple: This wood is a hardwood, and before you can successfully make burns across its surface, you will have to raise the pyrography pencil's temperature to a very high value. You will also have to keep the tip of the pen on the spot for longer seconds to last in burns.
3. Birchwood: This one has a light coloration that will make your burns stand out perfectly. It's one of the ideal wood types for wood burning!

4. Pine: Beginners mostly use this wood. It doesn't give any resistance when a pyrography pen tries to burn through it. However, before you use this for your artwork, make sure that it is properly dried in a kiln. The air-dried ones are usually prone to swellings across their surface, and that isn't too good for your work.

Sandpapers

It is with this essential material that you prep your wood for outlines on the surface. It is very wrong to burn across uneven surfaces! Even if you are a hundred percent confident that the wood is plane, still use sandpapers. That's exactly how important this step is.

Wrap the three hundred and twenty grit sandpaper around any wooden block and run it across the surface of the wood. Please, make sure you run the abrasive in the direction of the wood's grains. When you are done, wipe the dust off the wood's surface with a piece of dry fabric.

Even surfaces mean sharper outlines!

Now, here are a few tricks the sandpaper will do for you!

1. Sandpapers with fine grits work to eradicate oily stains or dangerous particles off the surface of your wooden board.
2. The ultrafine sandpaper will help you to get out soot from the tip of pyrography pens.
3. You can use sandpapers to scratch out mistakes made with light burns only. Errors made with dark burns may not be easily corrected by sandpapers.

Techniques involved in making the outlines of your design on a wooden board

There are several methods by which you can achieve this, and it all depends on how creative you are. Let's skim over a few of the techniques.

1. The freehand sketching.
2. Use of graphite or carbon paper
3. Use of a tracing paper.
4. Use of a transfer tip.

Freehand sketching is what you should go for if you feel you can handle pouring out your creative imaginations into a slab of wood. For example, this design technique will work best when dealing with complicated images that tracing will most definitely not work for. Drawing the face of a human being is one complicated image that requires freehand sketching.

However, for more straightforward sketches and designs, you can make use of the other options. However, make sure the picture of the image you want to design faces the graphite paper. Anything other than this will not fetch you any results.

Breath life into your work by adding colors

You can get colors from crayons, inks, and water-based colors. However, for beginners, it is advised that crayon is used since it is easier to handle. If you can control the other two's fluid nature, you should probably try them out.

Wipe off the mistakes

When you ate done burning and coloring, you can get rid of the extra lines and tracings. Sometimes, erasers do the trick, but then, the other times, you might have to source for alternatives.

There's one here for you, though. Sanding pens deal with errors tied to deep burns. These pens were initially designed to scratch off peeling paint off the bodies of vehicles. However, do not use this pen on softwood. It was designed to be used rigorously, and softwood cannot stand the pressure.

General tips!

- Make sure your workroom is well ventilated. The pyrography pen usually emits a lot of fumes that could irritate your eyes, so it'd be great if you got an expeller fan.
- To save your fingers from cramps, make sure you do not hold the pyrography pen too tightly. All you need to do is move your wrist fluidly to attain more profound levels of consistency.
- You can spray a finishing coating over your work to preserve the burn marks.

Chapter 3

Getting Started with Wood Burning

Now that you have an accurate idea of what wood burning means under the wide branch of pyrography, let's delve deeper into the process. Does this art involve me throwing in wood scraps into my kiln or fireplace? Or does it involve me writing on wood? If it's the latter, how possible is that?

Well, to get answers to all of your questions, you'll have to keep reading!

Basic Tools and Supplies Needed

Woodburning Pen

Woodburning pens have several parts like the rubber grip, the heat shield, the heating area, and the pen's tip. Two types of pen exist. One is a tool that operates with only one temperature. It's very great for beginners as it heats up to a temperature you set on it. It also has tips that can be easily changed. The variable temperature tool has a thermostat attached to it and tips that can either be fixed or changeable.

Razertip

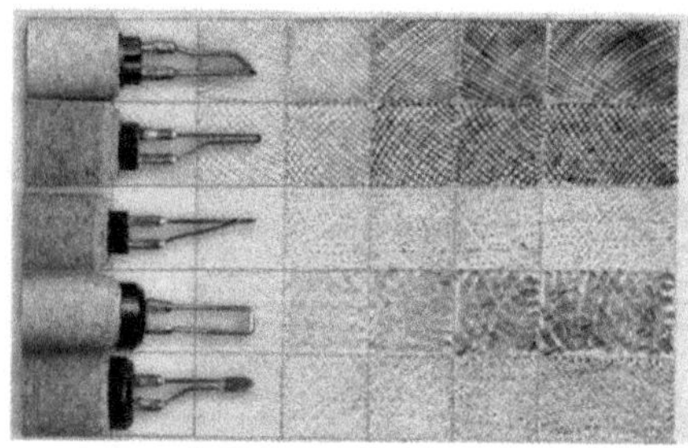

The pyrography pen tips include the flow tip, the universal tip, the calligraphic tip, the cone tip, and the large shading tip. Each of these tips has specific functions and outlines they are capable of burning.

Versa Tool

The versa tool is a tool that works under variable temperature settings and can be used to burn creative styles like whorls and curves into the wood.

Graphite or Carbon Paper

This is used in transferring designs to the wooden plaque. The back of the graphite sheet is dark, and so, it can easily leave imprints on the wood after a design has been traced against it.

Sandpaper

This is used to smoothen the surfaces of the wood. There are different sandpapers, all with different grits like 220, 150, 70, 80, etc.

Design to Wood-burn

A design is needed if you need your project to have a high degree of accuracy. This design is what you'll attach to the graphite paper and trace upon.

Helpful Accessories

Measuring Tape

This equipment is used to measure the length and breadth of the design and the wooden plaque. It will help a crafter to know whether the design will fit into the wood's surface or not.

Clear Tape

A clear tape is mostly used to fasten the design sheet and the graphite sheet together. You can also use it to hold the sheets to place while tracing out your design outlines.

Wet Paper Towel

Wet towels can be used to clean the tips of hot heating tools. You should also have this around so that you can easily use it to cool the area if you suffer a burn.

Red Ballpoint Pen

This pen is used for tracing the outlines of the design unto the wooden plaque.

Gloves

Wearing gloves will protect your fingers from the hot tips of the pyrography tool.

Dust Mask

When burning wood with the tip of a pyrography pen, there are usually thick fumes released. These fumes get even more dangerous when you are dealing with synthetic or reclaimed wood. Apart from these fumes, sanding a wooden surface may give rise to tiny dust particles that fill the air to the point of saturation. So, to protect your lungs, use a dust mask.

Knife Blade

This tool is used to add more intricate designs like wood carvings to your project. It helps to give your project intent and depth.

Scissors

You will use this tool to cut off anything that comes out of its borders.

Best Wood for Burning Wood Art

Like how a chef gets the best organic spices for whipping up food, crafters and pyrography artists also need the best wood for their projects. Wood is the base material needed for the woodburning art and you getting what'll bring out the beauty of your time and energy is what's most important.

Let's briefly discuss a few wood terms before finding out the best woods for wood burning.

1. Graining

Wood, as compact as it is, actually has grains that make it up! The grains of wood usually filed longitudinally are the patterns the wood fibers form as they grow. You know, before you got those wood plaques delivered to you, they once constituted to a tree. So, the direction of each wood cell is called the grain. The grain of a wood plaque also contributes to the texture of that wood.

Now, there are several kinds of graining arrangements wood can have. There's the straight grain, which by far is the commonest, the spiral grain, and the vertical grain. If you ever hear the word 'open grain,' know that it is related to each wood cell's size, i.e., the distance between those lines of fiber you see on wood. A wood plaque with densely packed grain lines is referred to as 'closely grained.' What these terms determine is whether or not a wood surface requires finishing touches to get it smooth.

So, now, what importance does the graining of wood have on your woodburning art? First, you have to be bothered about the direction or slope the grain lines tend to. It will help you know the direction you'll use your pyrography pen and sandpaper in. For example, if you use any of the tools in the same direction the grain tends to, you will surely get an articulate result. Since then, you won't be going against any lines; the operation will even come out smooth and easy.

Going against the grain lines may lead to bad occurrences like wood chips and tear-lines across the wood. However, you have to make your moves right-angled to the grain lines for some other wood trimming activities.

2. Reclaimed wood

This kind of wood is one that had undergone several degrees of processing and chemical treatments before it became whatever you see it as. This kind of wood can also be referred to as antique wood. They are mostly used in constructing things like cabinets, floors (do you remember the parquet floors?), and architectural set-ups.

3. Hardwood and softwood

Hardwood is obtained from plants that shed their leaves every year, while softwood is obtained from evergreen trees. The deciduous trees from which hardwood is obtained grow for very many years, and so, they usually have more densely packed wood-fibers than softwood. That's why hardwood is stronger than softwood.

Hardwood usually has a very dark color tone, while softwood has a very light color tone.

Hardwood is also one that has lower sap than softwood. Examples of hardwood include beech, maple, oak, poplar, balsa, hickory, mahogany, and walnut. Examples of softwood include cypress, fir, southern yellow pine, spruce, white pine, redwood, etc.

Now that you understand what the terms above mean, we can now delve into the kinds of wood you will find in the market and what's best for you to use in your woodburning art.

Poplar wood

This wood is commonly used by all artists that work with wood. It's almost everywhere you go, trust me. Why?

1. It's cheap wood with high quality! Honestly, it's really hard to find things that wrap these two features together. Most times, it's either cheap with very bad quality that affects your designs or that they have so high a quality that their prices come out terrifying.

2. It has a light color tone. This color tone is one feature you need to be looking out for in every wood you use. It will help push out your burn marks even more. Burn marks are dark already. Having them done on an already black surface only means you won't see your designs until you squint or get your glasses!

3. The grain arrangement is super duper great. When burning your designs through the wood, you can be assured you won't have to go through long hours trying to clear out some obstruction.

4. It is receptive to stains and keeps the color of the stain.

5. It is very easy to burn.

6. You can get this wood anywhere and at any time!

7. You can also get this wood in any size you want! You wouldn't know how serious this issue is until you get to the market. Most woods are only available in few dimensions.

8. The grains have the same soft texture. It never gets hard at some point; trust me.

So, in a wrap, the Poplar wood is what you should get as a beginner!

Maple

1. Maple is expensive, but then most crafters still rush to get it because of its very high quality. It is worth your every dime. Maple is the best wood anyone can ever use for wood burning.
2. It has a light color tone that brings out the dark burn patterns more beautifully than you'll ever imagine.
3. This wood has grains that you'll never really see until you draw your face closer to it. And this is very good as it gives you the impression of a plain and smooth working surface. It also doesn't affect how well the beauty of your work comes out eventually.
4. Now, before you get this wood, you have to get a high-quality pyrography pen that operates at high heat. Maple is a very hardwood that will require you exerting more force to get it burned through.

Beech

1. Do you need to be economical when getting your perfect wood? Well, this is one you can choose to go for.
2. It can easily serve as a substitute for the expensive maple or cheap poplar.
3. The beech wood is blessed with a light color tone.
4. It has a 'dash' pattern for its grain arrangement. The only issue this type of grain arrangement could cause is the leaking of sap when the wood is subjected to the pyrography pen's heat. So, if your work is eventually to be used for embellishing something, you'd not want to get this wood.

Jelutong

1. This wood is one that is used in diverse fields like wood carving. This is a plank of wood with high quality that can make your woodburning art the best thing ever.
2. If you will be burning into your wood with very intricate and stylish designs, you'd better go for this wood. It shapes all the curves nicely and helps you look professional.

Basswood

1. If you need a wood plaque that is extremely soft and easy to burn through, you should go for this. It is a wood type that is very excellent for wood burning.
2. The results of woodburning only get better when the wood has subtle grains. It makes your design literarily pop out of the wood.
3. It has a neat surface.
4. Basswood is light and portable.
5. Either you are working with a burn that comes out lightly or a burn that comes out darkly, you can use this wood.
6. You can get basswood in already cut plaque dimensions in most of the wood stores.

Birch

1. The grains are soft throughout.
2. It burns similarly to how basswood would.
3. It doesn't have resin or sap.
4. Birch is cheap to get
5. The beauty of using this wood is that the mistakes you make can be corrected easily.

6. However, you can't do any design that's too articulate or intricate on it as its fibers are densely joined together.

Oak

1. The kind of oak you will mostly find is the red oak.
2. The red oak is very hard to burn, and you might have to buy a very good pyrography pen to get your designs through it.
3. It has uneven wood grains.
4. Oak can be one of the most expensive things in the wood store.
5. Oak usually contains a lot of moisture that is certainly bad for your burning wood art. What's good for pyrography is wood that has been dried properly in a kiln.
6. It has too many grains that run prominently from side to side.

Pine

1. The kind of pine you will mostly find is the yellow pine.

2. Yellow pine is very common and available in almost every place.
3. Pine is very cheap!
4. The grains in yellow pine usually vary in texture and so, you may have a little difficulty getting it burned through. The grains also vary in color. The light ones are soft and won't pose a problem to you while you're burning. The darker ones, on the other hand, are hard. If you cannot deal with this inconsistency, you should try out another wood.

5. If you are burning a letter or shape into your wood, this wood is simply the best. It will help you bring out the outline beautifully
6. Yellow pine may not get you that beautiful and high-quality burn designs that you want, but then, you can always go for white pine.
7. White Pine is soft, easy to burn through, and gives your finished work a more rewarding look.

Pallet wood

1. Before purchasing this wood from the store, you must check if it is reclaimed wood. If it is, the chemicals in it may not go well with the heat. Inhaling these chemicals could cause respiratory issues you want to avoid. Most times, you will find it in reclaimed forms. So, check before buying.
2. It is easy to burn.
3. If you decide on using this, make sure you work in a place that allows for cross-ventilation, get an excellent fan that you can place close to your face, and lastly, wear a mask!

Walnut

1. Walnut is a hardwood that has a lot of grains across its surface.
2. You'll have to visit a lot of places before you can get this wood, and because it's scarce, the price could nearly get you taking to your heels. Surprisingly, it is much more expensive than Maple.
3. After adding your finishing touches, the wood begins to grow dark, and your burn marks become almost invisible.

4. Even with all the issues tied with this wood, it is very easy to burn across the surface.

Wood Panel

1. This wood is one that has already been sanded for you. So, when you get it, you can start burning through it almost immediately.
2. It has a light color tone.
3. The grain lines are few, and so your burnt outlines come out better.
4. You will also find this wood in any store.
5. The wood panel is available in several dimensions ranging from small ones like four by four inches and to large figures Luke forty-eight by seventy-two inches.

6. Ugly cases related to wood splintering doesn't exist with the wood panel.

Cherry

1. It has a non-uniform color distribution of grains.
2. It doesn't cost as much as Maple wood does.

3. Cherry is a hardwood, so its density and strength make it suitable for items or designs that should stand the test of time.
4. Cherry grows dark when the finishes are applied to the surface.

Alder

1. Alder is a hardwood with a very dark color tone that may not bring out the outline of your designs sharply.
2. Alder burns well since it lacks the obtrusive sap and resin.
3. You will find Alder everywhere. It's that common.
4. Alder is cheap to use.
5. Alder has very prominent grains that do more to hide the outlines of your design.
6. The Alder wood is only available in a few plaque sizes. Most of the plaque sizes are just about four inches wide.

Hickory

1. Every wood out there has a design it is very good in. For hickory, it is the area of decorating that it

features well in. Other aspects may be a zero for it.

2. It is a hardwood that's just as dark as chocolate!
3. The grain patterns are very prominent.
4. The only reason this wood might be suitable for wood burning is that it lacks sap and resin.

Butternut

1. Butternut makes a nice background for your design projects.
2. You can get butternut in already set shapes.
3. It is available almost in every woodshop.
4. It has a special kind of grain that does not appear too prominently on your project.
5. It has a beige color.
6. When varnished with polyurethane, it glows with a silvery effect.

Types of Woods to Avoid

When looking for what will work best for your woodburning art, ensure that you avoid buying dark woods that won't project your design burns, woods with prominent graining, and woods with too much resin and sap.

Stay away from woods with rough surfaces!

Do not purchase reclaimed wood that has been furnished heavily with chemicals or any other synthetic material. When heat is applied to these kinds of wood, they release very dangerous vapors that you should not be inhaling!

Take note that softwoods have fewer grains than hardwoods, so if you are looking for something very to burn through, go for softwoods. Choose the soft and easy wood to burn through because that way, you are faced with lesser complications and energy losses.

Choose wood whose density ranges between three inches to eight inches! Woods with almost no density at all end up bending at the sides. The only exception is plywood. It can be easily destroyed by water.

Wood Burning Safety Rules

As wonderful and interesting as this art is, it sadly has many dangers and risks attached to it that can easily get you discouraged. So, as a crafter or pyrography artist, you just have to ensure that you are very careful. There could be fire hazards, heat, skin irritation, breathing difficulties, burns, and many other issues that you have to make sure you prevent as much as possible.

Let's start with the pyrography pen. A pen is a heating tool whose blade can be so hot that your fingers get badly scalded if they ever come in contact with it. Imagine, even wood gets burnt on touching this hot blade to the point that fumes rise from it! To avoid getting your skin burnt, make sure you do the following.

1. Wear thick gloves when handling the pen so that your fingers are protected even if the blade mistakenly touches them.
2. Keep your device plugged out of the socket when you are not using it! This will go a long way to ensure that the blade isn't just spending time getting as hot as a furnace!
3. If the heating device has a long cord, connect it in such a way that it does not obstruct your passageways. You know, you could be in so much hurry at a moment that you'd forget that there was a cord right in front of you. Now, once you trip on it, your weight could pull the hot pyrography pen off your working table and then cause it to land on your skin! Be careful.
4. Pyrography pens usually come with racks where you can keep inclined against if you ever need to

drop them while working. Use them and don't place your pen just anywhere on your working desk.

5. Do not hold the pen at the tip where it is hot. Wrap your fingers instead of the paddings provided for grip.

6. To prevent fire hazards, ensure that you plug in your pyrography tool into a good socket that will supply the right amount of current to it. Also, when you see that the device is too hot for comfort, turn it off and allow it to rest against its rack.

The next thing you should be careful with is the kind of wood you use! Most of the woods have had their natural properties replaced with artificial ones by polishes, stains, and chemical finishing sprays. All of these things can lead to the creation of harmful fumes when the wood is burnt. So, to avoid unnecessary complications, do the following.

1. Ensure that you do your study on how toxic the wood type you are getting is before actually going on to purchase it. If it is toxic, please, discard the thought of using it. Luckily for you,

several other kinds of wood can be a better substitute for the toxic one.

2. Ensure that the wood you are getting isn't one that allows a lot of sawdust to float around in the air. Sawdust is tiny articles that could easily find their way through your mouth, nose, lungs, and ears and then cause irritation internally. This could eventually pose some serious tract diseases. Apart from having issues with your respiratory tract, having sawdust land on your skin can cause it to get irritated to a large extent.

3. Even if the wood you plan on getting comes out toxic-free after conducting your research, ensure that it is also risk-free.

4. Work in properly ventilated areas.

5. Keep your windows open!

6. Get a fan that will work effectively to blow away the fumes. This way, the fumes don't have to go right through your nose.

7. Stay away from wood plaques that have been coated with paint and chemicals. Even if you decide to sand them all off, you may never know how deeply the chemicals have penetrated the wood, so just help yourself and stay away. Some

examples of these kinds of woods are medium density fiberboard and plywood. The former contains formaldehyde, which is very harmful to you. On the other hand, the latter can pose a lot of risk to you if you burn through the wood so deeply that you reach the glue.

8. If you live in the outskirts of the town where many trees are, you can be sure to find a local woodshop. You can make a few arrangements with the people there to get newly cut wood.

General safety rules

1. As a beginner, make sure you watch as many videos as possible to help you know what you should be doing and the things you shouldn't. It will save you from wasting your time, energy, and money. Before you even take on big projects, make sure you get familiar with the pyrography tool. This will help you get used to making ridges, lines, burns, and curves with your pen.

2. Make sure you allow the temperature of the blades to reduce considerably before you change them. And that can happen within five minutes if

the tool's heat wasn't too high before you turned it off.

3. Burn the wood slowly to make sure that there is consistency in your wood burning projects. If you want deep black burns, go slowly, and if you want light burns, you can quicken your pace, but only a bit.

4. Keep a moist towel beside you as you work as well as an ointment for burns.

In cases where you suffer a burn, what do you do? First, you'll notice that the area gets red, and even though it might feel numb for the first few minutes, the pain still ends up coming sharply. Instead of just doing nothing, follow the following guidelines.

1. Run cool water over the burning surface so that the heat of the pain reduces a bit. You can also use a cool towel to press down on the part of your hand where the burn occurred.

2. To promote blood circulation, pull out any ring, bracelet or wristwatch you have on. Be sure to do this as soon as possible. If the burned area ends up swelling, pulling the items out might be difficult and painful.

3. If the area swells with fluid, do not burst it by tearing the softened skin. The fluid keeps infections out of the burned areas. If it bursts for any reason, use water or a bar of very gentle soap to clean the spot. After that, rub in an antibiotic ointment that will do the job of the fluid that broke out.

4. To ease yourself of the searing pain, rub in Aloe Vera or any other moisturizer on the spot.

5. Once that is done, loosely wrap a sterile bandage around the burn to keep air away from it. The bandage minimizes the pain and also shields the blister.

6. You can also reduce the pain by taking pain killers like ibuprofen and acetaminophen.

Preparing Wood for a WoodBurning Art

Once you get your wood from the store, the next thing you need to do is to prepare it for wood burning. However, you can skip this phase if you purchased wood plaques like a wood panel that has already been worked on for you.

If the edges of the wood you want to work on aren't as smooth as you want them to be, you use a saw or any other cutting tool you have to cut off the uneven edges. Then, you can use the sandpaper to smoothen out the rough edges. Do not run the sandpaper up and down the length of the wood, though. This could cause the wood to chip off, and that will ruin the whole thing. Instead, follow the transverse lines and run your sandpaper block towards the outer edges.

To solve the issue of dents and irregularities on your wood surface, you can just get a thick and slightly moist towel. Place it on the dent and then use a hot iron to press the cloth down to the dent. This procedure will help the irregularities to align with the regular surface of the wood.

Now, follow the procedures below to get your wood plaque ready for burning:

1. Decide on what sandpaper you want to use. To start the process, you can decide to use the sandpaper in a progressive order. So, you can start with the one with 50 grits, continue with the one with 60 grit, 80 grit to prepare the wood.

2. Wrap the sandpaper you want to use around a box. This will help you apply firmer pressure on the wood while you are getting it sanded. It will also increase the surface area of wood the sandpaper rubs against per swipe of your hand.
3. Sand the wood to a surface coating of about 220 grit.
4. The next thing is to get the wood surface to have a moist feel. So, to get the wood wet, you can get a moist towel and rub it across the surface. This will help you get rid of the particles released on the surface due to the sanding. You aren't supposed to make the surface of the wood drip with water, though.
5. Set the plaque aside for a few minutes for the moisture on it to dry.
6. Once it is dry, use the 220grit sandpaper to make the surface even smoother.
7. Now, the wood is ready for you to draw your designs on.

Another reason the water was spread across the wood's surface was so that the grains could bulge out of the wood a little. When you use the sandpaper again, the surface would be as smooth as the body of an egg. Smooth surfaces are very important in woodwork because then, the burning tool's blades do not face any opposition as they burn through the wood. Also, your designs end up coming out even better than you can ever imagine.

Transferring a Woodburning Pattern onto the Wood

After preparing your wood, the next issue is finding the right image to imprint on the wooden surface. This step may not be completely necessary if you plan on using your creativity in drawing out your designs on the surface of the wood. But then, if you cannot risk doing that or you perhaps want a very accurate design, ensure that while searching for an image, you get something whose dimensions fit into the size of the wood plaque. You should also consider getting images in black and white print so that you can easily lay it on the wooden board.

After getting the image from the internet or print it out with a black and white printer, to get the outlines fixed on the wood, you will need a graphite or carbon paper and a transfer tip (preferably the tips of pens that are no longer functioning.

The next thing you need to do is align your graphite paper with the image. Then, cut off the excesses. Keep the two sheets together with tape. Meanwhile, ensure that the dark side of the graphite paper is pressed to the wood so that you can easily see the outlines when you remove it.

Now, you can begin to trace the image. While tracing, ensure that the transfer tip only runs across the edges you want to see on your wood. For the areas you see shaded in the picture, you need not trace them. It will help your outlines to be neater. Besides, you can always shade those areas once you are done with the whole thing by looking at the picture.

Once you are done, lift the graphite paper and the image to view what you have traced. Do well to ensure that the tape joining the graphite paper with the image does not get removed. It will help you in cases where you notice that there are some lines you missed. However, if you see any errors or marks that ought not to be on the board, you can easily wipe them off with sandpaper or eraser.

After this procedure, you can proceed to the next level, which involves passing the pyrography pen through the outlines. To get deep and long-lasting burns, ensure that you press the blade harder to the outlines. However, to start burning the wood, ensure you make all the outlines have dark shades before continuing later to darken the lines. If you are burning through hardwood like Maple, you might need to increase the pen's heat to the highest. This will help you form consequential and prominent burns on the wood.

The pyrography pen usually comes with different blades, and each blade works for a particular function. Some blades help you to burn through straight lines, to burn through curvy lines, circles and also, to shade. So, you can choose anyone you want. Most importantly, before you start any woodwork project, make sure you must have practiced using the tool earlier on.

Coloring a Woodburning Project

You'd honestly be surprised at how much effect color can add to your woodwork designs! Instead of the boring black burns, you can get various colors, lighting every curve and edge. Wood burning and color applications are a match made in heaven. You don't want ever to miss them!

Coloring your project will help take your mind off your anxieties, cares, worries, and sadness. Instead, you get to fill your mind with vivid imaginations, green ideas, and most importantly, peace. Your project could even heal a distressed person. Don't you believe it? Try it first.

The following are the things that you can use to color your project.

1. Markers.
2. Myriad shades of wood staining products.
3. Chalk or pastels.
4. Crayons.
5. Food dye.
6. Oil paints.
7. Colored pencils.
8. Acrylic paints.

The other accessories that you will need include:

1. Pencils
2. Brushes
3. Alcohol
4. Eraser
5. Col wood detailer

Before you go on with coloring your projects, you need to know a few things that will help your work come out even more nicely.

- You have to apply the colors first on some sheet of paper or scrap of wood that you don't need anymore. This way, you can think of harmonizing, balancing, unifying, and creating the needed contrast between the colors you will work with. Making mistakes on the real wood plaque can be very costly, so you have to do all you can to avoid it by practicing ahead of the real deal.

- Try as much as possible to stay away from using water-based paints. Allowing water on your woodwork will only push the grain out of the wood surface, and that can prevent your project from standing out of the wood. Instead, you can just go for watercolor pencils. After applying them to your woodwork projects, you can create glossy effects by moistening them with alcohol. This way, they get dissolved into paints and then go deep into the wood fibers' link, giving your deep work feelings of resonance.

- If you need your colors to blend nicely with the wood you used, work with light colors to give an impression of transparency to the project. This way, you can succeed in striking at deep levels of naturalness.

How to apply colors on your woodwork projects

- Sharpen the edges of the watercolor pencils before using them on the woodburning project.

- Color lightly first before you proceed to color darkly. This will help you a lot since errors that have to do with dark coloring can be easily avoided.

- When you finish coloring lightly, darken the areas you want to create impressions like contour, shadows, and other dark hues.

- Pour a little bit of alcohol in a bowl, dip the brush's tufts in it, and then use it to brush across the surfaces.

- Allocate brushes to every color you used to avoid an issue of color smudging.

- Allow the wood plaque to dry.

Using acrylic paints to color your wood burning projects will help you paint thinly or thickly. It will help get you the right layers of colors and make color blending as easy as ABC. Acrylic paint is very easy to control and works on the surface of any wood plaque.

Sealing the Finished Project

Sealing your woodwork projects help the colors you used on it to come out even better. Also, you wouldn't have to worry about your project getting marred with scratches, dents, dirt, and oil stains. It will also help give your project a finer and more refined look.

Sealing your wood burning project is the last thing you'll do in the long list of procedures. Just like the word 'seal' means, you get to seal your burn outlines with finishing sprays and, in a way, preserve their quality. However, when finishing up your works with seals, do it so that it will not hide the burn outlines from the viewers' eyes. You should aim for something that you can still see through eventually.

You will need a brush you can use to spread the finish or varnish across the surface for this last step. To cover a larger wood area in a shorter time, you must use the normal large square-shaped paintbrush. For finishes that exist as sprays, all you need to get is a container with spray handles.

Lint-free cloths are special pieces of fabric with thin fibers that will easily eradicate wood dust and eraser peels that stick to the wood.

Things to do before sealing a wood burn project

1. Lightly run a sandpaper block with fine grits along the surfaces of your woodwork project. You will see the importance of this step when you run your fingers across the wood's surface with the burn marks. The burning procedure usually leaves the fibers bulging out roughly a bit. To do this, you can make use of emery boards with foam cores. These kinds of boards are sandpapers that are available in different kinds of grits. They are cheap and can be found in as many wood stores as you can find.
2. After running the emery board across the wood's surface to smoothen out the rough surfaces, use an eraser to clean off the other unnecessary lines from the outlines and burns.

3. To get the eraser peels and sawdust off the board, use a piece of fabric free from lint.

4. After smoothening the surfaces and erasing the unnecessary lines and burns, you can now get ready to seal the wood with any finish of your choice!

Examples of finishers and their usefulness

Spray polyurethane

This finisher is a general-purpose sealant that does not affect your wood burns or the colors you applied to it. If you used this method to seal your designs, you could finish in less than thirty minutes! Whether or not you can use this particular method of preserving your artwork's quality is hardly ever affected by the kind of coloring you used.

The polyurethane is usually sprayed across the surface of your wood burn projects, so of course, it doesn't have to mess up with anything you have taken your time to do. This sealant exists in high gloss, gloss, and semi-matte forms. Knowing which to go for all depends on how thickly you want your design to be sealed.

Before you rush to seal your work thickly, begin with very light sprays across the surface of the wood. Then, leave that to dry. If you are satisfied with that, you can just leave it like that. However, if you aren't, apply another thin layer of the sealant.

Not all forms of polyurethane are in the forms of aerosols, though. There's the liquid form that you can apply to the surface of your wood burn projects with a brush that is ultra-soft and free of residual paint. You could also use the guidelines to help you work well with this form of sealant.

Oil finish

Have you perhaps been looking for something fantastic that will bring out the naturalness of the wood grains and the beauty of your burn marks? The oil finish method of sealing your project is great as it allows it to stand the test of time!

The three types of oils used in this kind of finish are the Tung oils, Danish oils, and Linseed oil. Applying them to the surface of your wood would be great if you follow through with the manufacturer guidelines.

Dip your soft brush into the oily finish, and then run it across the wooden surface to start. Leave the wood plaque for about fifteen to twenty minutes so that the oil coats into something thick. To eliminate the excessive oil layers that refuse to dry even after that time, use a cloth material that is free from lint to wipe it off.

Since oil doesn't dry as quickly as water does, you may have to leave the sealed wooden plaque till the next day to allow it to dry. After you are sure it has dried completely into something glazy, you can now use a brush to apply another layer of the oil finish. After this second layer dries, you will have successfully succeeded in sealing the product.

All the oils listed above, apart from Linseed oil, can pose really serious problems to an individual's health. Linseed is, to an extent, safe to be used with food, but then, most times, it doesn't stand the test of time. Most times, linseed oil is applied on the surfaces of cutting boards and over wooden kitchen equipment. And so, because of this sealant, you can avoid cases that involve the warping or cracking of the wood you used for constructing the board.

Paste wax

To use this sealant, you must follow the guidelines on the surface of the can. Dab any piece of lint-free cloth in the paste wax and then run it across the whole surface of the wooden plaques.

After spreading the paste wax evenly about the surface, please leave it to dry for about ten to fifteen minutes. When the paste wax dries, it changes into a white opaque layer that tends to hide your project's burn marks. To get rid of this, use a soft piece of clothing to rub the coating surface until it shines out like glass.

You can apply more layers of the paste wax if you aren't satisfied with the thickness of the one you already have. In many cases, too many layers of paste wax could cause your project to end up with a look that blurs your wood burn designs. To get rid of that cloudiness, use a piece of fabric to eliminate the excess wax.

However, it is unfortunate that the paste wax cannot stand the test of time like polyurethane can as most times, it either gets cloudy or fades off to expose your real artwork designs. The one reason the paste wax is commonly used is because of its distinctive glow. However, it does little or nothing to protect your woodburning from scratches, oil, moisture, and heat.

Ultraviolet ray inhibitors

Sunlight is one real enemy of pyrography. Even if you were to place a scrap of wood in the sun for days, you would notice how much paler the wood will turn out to be. So, if your woodburning project is one that will be put out in the sun for a lot of hours, you really should consider using sealants with UV-ray inhibitors in them.

The commonest ultraviolet inhibitor out there is spar urethane, and coincidentally, it is the one form of polyurethane that lasts for long.

Lacquer

Lacquer is a finishing sealant that doesn't turn yellow as time passes. It also dries off pretty quickly when you apply it to the surface of the wood. And in case you make a mistake while using lacquer, you can easily use a thinner that will remove the excess glossy layers. However, ensure the room you work in is well ventilated while working with the lacquer finish since the smell could be somewhat concentrated.

The other varnishes that you can use for your project include Jung oil and Danish oil. These oils are food-friendly and so, you can use them to finish the surfaces of your serving trays and cooking utensils. After sealing your wood burn project, you should ensure that you take adequate caution by keeping it from places with high temperatures and dirt.

Cleaning Your Woodburning Projects

Over time, there is a tendency that your project gets stained with either dirt, oil, or dust. The wood you used could also undergo serious color changes as the wood gets oxidized by the air's free gases. This is why a scrap of white pine will end up getting darkened to a light brown color. This issue of color change is called Patina.

You will have to clean your woodburning projects when a disturbing layer of dirt spreads across the surface of your project. The dust could even find its way into the very intricate grooves, curves, and carvings, thereby killing the beauty and glow of your project.

Things to know before cleaning your woodwork project;

1. Only use a concentrated wood cleaner that won't pose a health problem to people and animals.
2. Ensure that the cleaner you get won't get your sealant to erode.
3. Before using any wood cleaner on your woodwork project, ensure that your first use it at

the bottom of the wood plaque so that you can
check out for any reaction or damage it could
cause to the wood.

Follow the following steps to clean your woodburning
projects:

1. Use a damp cloth to wipe the dust off the surface
   of the wood plaque.
2. If the dust has eaten deep into the grooves, make
   use of devices that blow out air from their holes
   to get rid of the dust.
3. Add one cup of the wood cleaner to about two
   cups of warm water.
4. Get a toothbrush to scrub the grooves, a big shoe
   brush to scrub the surface of the wood, and begin
   to work the soapy solution on the wood surface.
5. The more stubborn dirt gets removed too. It
   would help if you allowed the soapy solution to
   remain on the surface for some minutes.
6. When the dirt has been scrubbed out, tilt it to the
   side so that the soapy fluid slides off the surface.
7. Next thing you should do is use a dry cloth free
   from lint to wipe the wood surface until it's dry.

Do not use water to get rid of the soap as it can lead to further complications.

8. If you aren't satisfied, you can repeat the above steps.

To clean your tools, follow the steps below;

1. Use Aluminum oxide to clean the tips of your tool. This method works for both one-temperature and variable temperature tips. Just place little of the honing compound on a sheet of paper, and then, drag the tip of the tool across it. You can repeat this process as many times as possible until the tip is free from carbon deposits. This method of cleaning the tip of your heating pen is very good since it doesn't damage the tips. Apart from that, you can be assured of getting cleanly burned lines after using this method.

2. For pens with variable temperature tips, some of them come with the manufacturer's scraping tool. This tool has a pointed mouth that you can drag across the pen's tip to get rid of the carbon deposits.

<u>A Short message from the Author:</u>

Hey, I hope you are enjoying the book? I would love to hear your thoughts!

Many readers do not know how hard reviews are to come by and how much they help an author.

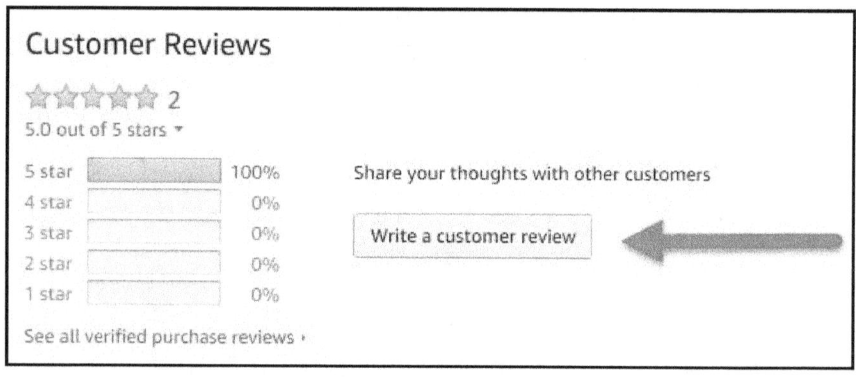

I would be incredibly grateful if you could take just 60 seconds to write a short review on Amazon, even if it is a few sentences!

>> Click here to leave a quick review

Thanks for the time taken to share your thoughts!

Chapter 4

Woodburning Project Ideas to Wood-burn

Now, it's time for you to be creative! It's time for you to exercise those fingers to create the most beautiful things ever! You can start by burning up something nice for your friend. You could even use your fantastic projects as gift items. Do you know how much smile you'll put on the face of the person that receives such a gift? Besides, you could use it to give your house this cool medieval feel that will get all your visitors permanently awed! Do you want to try this out? Then, let's get started!

Clock

Have you ever thought about making a clock carved out of wood? No? Try this out now!

Supplies needed

- Basswood.
- A pyrography pen.
- Clock accessories.
- Figures in different fonts.
- Tape.

- Pencil.
- Wood stains.
- Glue.

Steps Involved

1. After deciding what font or design to use for the numbers that'll be on your clock, print it out in a black and white style and then cut it.
2. Since the cuttings would be too small, attaching a graphite paper behind it may be extraneous. So, you can shade the back of the cut sheets completely with a deep black lead pencil. Make sure the shadings extend throughout the corners of the sheet.
3. If you already haven't carved the basswood into the shape you want, do it now!
4. Arrange the cut sheets of paper at the places you want them to be in. For example, place '12' at the side that's supposed to be the top, '6' at the bottom, '3' by the right side, and '9' by the left side. You can decide to fix something for the other numbers too, but then, there's a possibility

the whole board gets clumsy. You certainly do not want that.

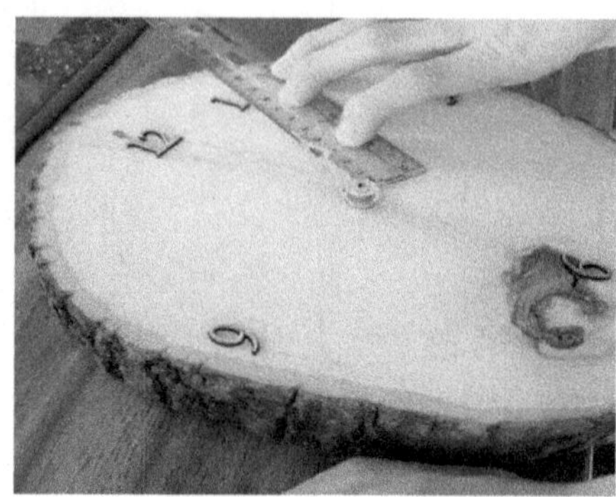

5. Now, you can begin to trace the figures' outlines against the already prepped surface of your basswood.
6. Once you are done with everything, you'll see the lead markings on the wood's surface.
7. Now, it's time to burn those figures into the wood
8. Grab your pyrography pen and get it plugged into a reliable source of power.
9. Since basswood is hardwood, you might have to turn on the heat settings to the highest levels to get a deep burn.
10. Touch up your project with the wood stains you got.

11. Leave your clock to dry! It would be best if you didn't put it out under the sun, though, because sunlight has a bad effect on wood.
12. Fix the other parts of the clock to your project once it dries. And those other parts to include the motor and the hands of the clock. You are done!

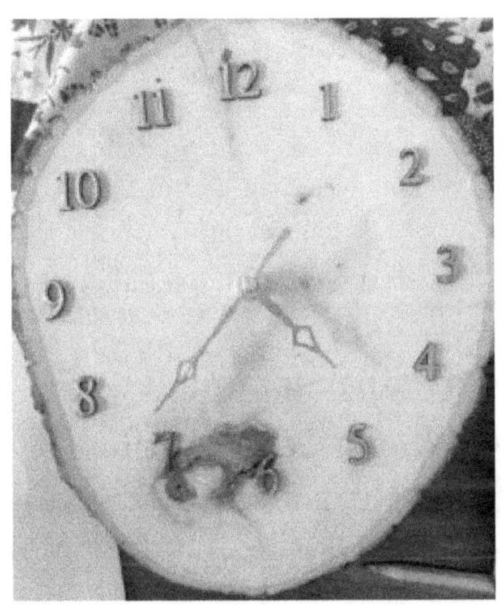

Serving Boards

How beautiful would it be to decorate your wooden serving boards yourself? Even as you place your plates of food on it, there's this sense of pride and excitement that fills you! Let's just get started already.

Supplies needed

- A large wooden serving board.
- Versa tool.
- An abrasive (sandpaper)
- A soft rag.
- Pencil.
- Eraser.
- Linseed oil.

Steps Involved

1. Wrap the sandpaper around a wooden box.
2. Run the abrasive across the wooden board's surface to get it smooth and ready for burning! It'd be nice if you used the 220-grit sandpaper, though.
3. Use the rag to dust off the specks of dust raised by the sanding processes from the wooden plaque.

4. To your Versa tool, change the blade to one that works for shading. Power the device and wait for the temperature of the blade to rise.

5. While waiting, you can quickly sketch the outline of your design across the corners of your board. It could be weaved flowers, several circles, anything! Just ensure that it's something that'll catch the eye.

6. Now, run the heated blade of the Versa tool across the outlines lightly. You wouldn't want to start with dark burns because then, you wouldn't be able to correct any mistake you might make. So, to make light burns, do not leave the tip of the blade on the spot for too long.

7. After doing this, use your eraser to clean off the unnecessary lines. Do not use colored erasers. They could leave horrible marks on your board that you certainly will not like.

8. You can draw more outlines if you want to decorate the board some more. For example, at the center, you could draw circles and curves, run the Versa tool blade along the lines, and embellish it with something even fancier and shade!

Once you are done, use the Linseed oil to coat the wood surface. Linseed oil is a wood-friendly oil that gives the surface of your wood a brilliant sheen. However, make sure you do not use these boards after sealing with the oil as platters for cutting. It may ruin the whole thing.

Dragon

This is a wonderful project idea for those who desire to take wood burning to a higher level. You could put it up in a museum or display it at the exhibition grounds in your school.

Supplies needed

- A ten by ten-inch basswood plaque.
- A copy of the dragon design of a seven by seven-inch dimension.
- A pyrography pen of variable heat settings.
- Graphite sheet or carbon paper.
- A tape.
- Fine grit sandpaper or foam-core emery boards.
- Polyurethane or Paste wax finish.
- Lint-free cloth.

- Pencils.
- Erasers.
- Tracing paper.
- Transfer tips.

Steps Involved

1. Attach the finely gritted sandpaper to a box of wood.
2. Use the box-shaped abrasive to rub across the surface of the wood.
3. Wipe off the sand dust with a lint-free fabric.
4. Fix the graphite paper to the copy of the dragon design with tape and then place it on the basswood's surface. Make sure that the side that faces the wood is the dark side of the graphite paper. This will go a long way to ensure that your outlines are fixed nicely to the wood.
5. You can now start to trace your design's needed outlines with a non-functional ballpoint pen. Do not bother to trace shadows or the dark shadings on the original design copy. Remember, you need clean details that will help with the burning process.

6. Peel off the board sheets and then erase any confusing or extraneous lines with a white eraser. Colored erasers will only leave terrible markings on your wood that you want to avoid.

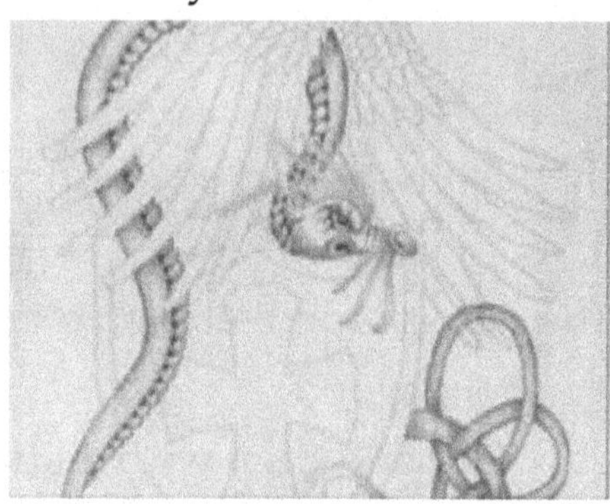

7. Now, it is time to begin the shading process. Get your shading tool, heat it, and begin to run it lightly across the lines. Start with the bold details first before moving on to the more intricate ones. Make sure that you regularly clean the tip of your blade as you proceed.

8. Start from the top of the dragon's body and finish at the bottom. You might have to change the tips of your pen to burn the areas that need burning.

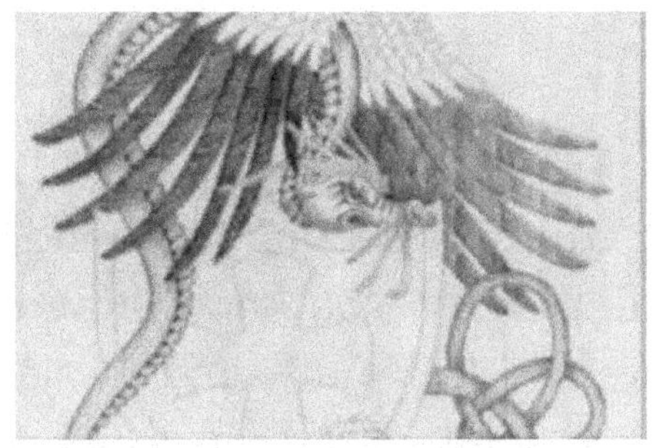

9. When you are done, run sandpaper across the surface of your wood project. You could also use a foam-core emery board to smoothen the rough surfaces.

10. Now, since this job requires a lot of meticulousness, tilt it against something and observe it closely. See if the dark tones blend with the light ones. If you don't see that sharp contrast, you can continue with the project by adding more shadows or shades to bring out the beauty.

11. After seeing to it that everything is balanced, sand the surface lightly again and then wipe off the wood dust with a lint-free cloth.

12. Seal your project with a finish like polyurethane or paste wax. If the project is going to be displayed outside, you should use polyurethane and some ultraviolet inhibitor.

Pendants for Necklace

You have that cultural meeting to attend, and yet, you still use a golden chain! You know how to wood burn, and yet, you refuse to flaunt your projects? Stop that immediately and craft up your own beautiful and natural pendant that will leave people staring at you forever!

Supplies needed

- Basswood.
- Pyrography pen.
- Sandpaper.
- Water-color pencils
- Alcohol
- Pencils.
- Erasers.

Steps Involved

1. Carve the basswood into whatever shape you want your pendant to be in. You could decide to go with octagonal shaped pendants, circular

pendants, or rectangular pendants. It all depends on you!

2. After carving the wood into the shape you want, use sandpaper to smoothen the wood's sides and edges. Make sure you run the abrasive in the direction of the wood's grains so that the wood will not get chipped along the surfaces

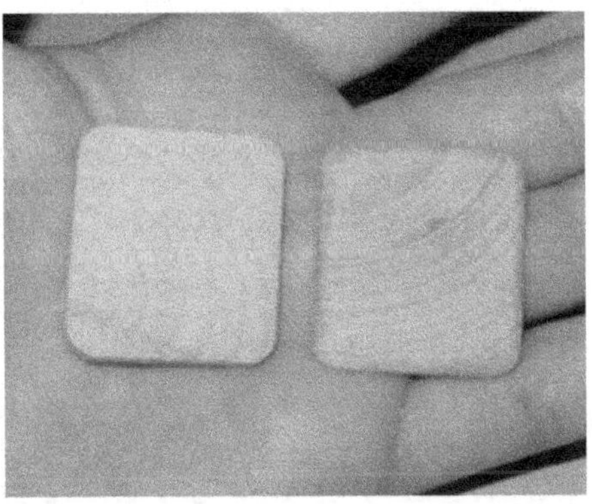

3. When you are done, use a lint-free cloth to clean the wood dust off the surface.
4. You can then use a pencil to outline whatever thing you want to see on the surface of the

pendant. It could be the outline of a feather, flower, or even a plain sphere.

5. Once you finish drawing, use a white eraser to wipe off the extraneous lines and shades.

6. Now, plug in your heating tool and make sure the blade is the solid tipped one that will help you but big and bold lines.

7. Run the tip of the blade across the outlines lightly at first before deepening the effect. Starting with deep burns can be very bad, especially when you have to correct a mistake. Lighter errors can easily be corrected with an eraser or sandpaper, unlike dark burns. Also, since you will be making something that will be out for everyone to see, make sure you are calm and collected as you run the blade across the design outline. It will help your work to look smooth and neat.

8. When you are done, use sandpaper to smoothen the grains that may have been pushed to the surface by the burn marks. Remember, you want the surface to look as neat as possible.

9. Now, if you want, you can decide to add color to your work. Simply sharpen your watercolor pencils and then use the edges to color the burns

of your design deeply. Water-based colors may push the wood's grain out of the leveled surface, which cannot be good.

10. To give it a glossy appearance, dip a soft brush inside a small bottle of alcohol. Then, run it across the already colored designs.
11. Leave your pendant to dry.
12. Once it is dry, you can sand it finely again to make it thoroughly smooth.
13. Use a drilling tool to make a hole at the top of the pendant. After that, you can pass in a chain of cowries or a chain of something else that gives cultural vibes through the loop.
14. Your necklace is ready!

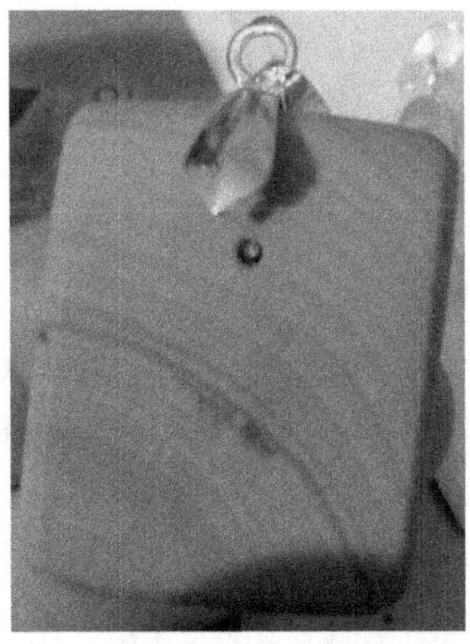

Rainbow Roses

This is another big wood burning project that you want to try out. You can display this in an art gallery or even use it to decorate your home! Brilliant, right?

Let's get our hands busy!

Supplies needed

- A pyrography pen.
- A wooden plaque of basswood material.
- Graphite paper or carbon paper
- Tape
- Pencils
- Eraser
- Pastel paint pens or watercolor pencils
- Alcohol
- A shading tool.

Steps Involved

1. Smoothen the surface of the wood with a fine gritted sandpaper. The sandpaper will help you to smoothen the sides and edges of the wood. You should also make sure you run the abrasive in the direction of the wood's grains so that the wood will not get chipped along the edges.

2. If you feel you are skilled enough, you can run the rose's outline with your free hand. Draw as many whorls as possible, each with a shape that protrudes out of the center.

3. However, if you feel you need a high degree of accuracy in your work, get a design sample. Attach a graphite paper to the back of the design sheet and then fix it to the board. Ensure that it's the dark side of the graphite paper that faces the board, though.

4. Now, use a transfer tip to trace the outlines and edges of the design. When you are done, peel it off the surface.

5. Now, you can plug in your heating tool and then wait for the blade to get hot.

6. Start burning the inner whorls of the flower first before moving on to the outer ones. It'd be very good if you used a heating tool with a penciled mouth to line the insides, though.

7. Ensure that your hand is so steady that the burn marks do not pass out of the lines. This will contribute immensely to you having a very neat project.

8. For the outer whorls, let your burns be deeper and thicker.

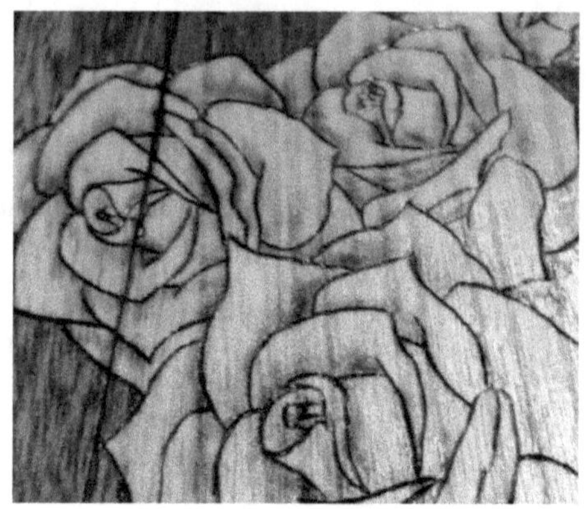

9. When you are done burning, you can use your shading tool to apply shadows and dark contours to the design's outermost and innermost edges. This step won't be necessary, though, if you will be painting at the end.

10. Now, it's time to attend to the rainbow aspect of this design and to do that, you can either use pastel paint or watercolor pencils. Here, we will use pastel paint because of the effects of contrast we will make on the design. However, if you use watercolor pencils, it's all okay. All you just need to do is rub in alcohol around the surfaces to create a glossy appearance.

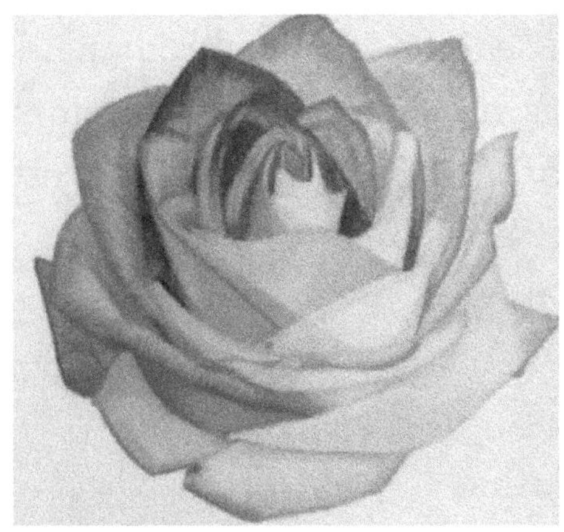

11. So, we'll start with the same base of all the flower whorls for the pastel paint.
12. Use all of the colors of pencils here to create a nice scenario of contrast and harmony in your project.
13. As you proceed to the other whorls, use brighter colors. The rainbow colors are red, orange, yellow, green, blue, indigo, and violet.
14. At the edges, work in contrast by using your thumbs to create a gradual rise in color tone.
15. When you are done coloring, blending, and harmonizing, you can lightly run the tip of your burning pen across the lines of the whorls to accentuate them.
16. Allow your project to dry.

17. You can seal it with polyurethane. It is one finish that does not mess with the colors you used in your work. Make sure that you use a foam-core emery board to sand the surface lightly before sealing, though.

Welcome Wreaths

You could place a welcome wreath right at the entrance of your house to give whoever is visiting this feeling of excitement and peace. Apart from this, the wreaths can also help to brighten your house's interiors or exteriors. Let's get started.

Supplies needed

- Basswood carved into circular sizes.
- A pyrography pen.
- A shading tool
- Drills.
- Pencils
- Erasers
- Ultraviolet inhibitors.

Steps Involved

1. Sand the surface of the circular basswood plaques with a finely gritted sandpaper. This procedure will prepare the surface for the next step. It will also prevent any form of obstruction when you are working your heating tool through the wood's surface. By the way, you will need seven of these sanded platters, each for one letter in the word, 'WELCOME.'

2. Draw the letterings on each surface of the wood in different font styles.

3. If you cannot risk drawing it with your free-hand, you can use graphite or carbon paper to transfer your design to the wood.

4. Erase the unnecessary lines and return the sheets to the wood if there were some lines you missed.

5. Once you have the outline of your design ready, run the blade of your pyrography pen through the outlines to burn through the wood. Since the wreath is for everyone to see, you can take your time to achieve deep burns that shine out of the pale wood.

6. Add shadows and dark layers to give the burnt letters a new look and definition. To do this, use your shading tool.

7. Once you burn the outlines on each wood plaque, sand the surface lightly with fine sandpaper to smooth the surface.

8. Since the plaques of wood might be exposed to sunlight, there could be a possibility that it gets pale due to oxidation. So, ensure that you spray the surface with a finish that contains UV inhibitors.

9. The next step involves you drilling in two holes in your small wood plaques, each one by the side. Once you get this done, you can pass a string through the holes to create something that looks closely like a necklace.

10. You can tie a colorful ribbon to the wreath to beautify your project even more.

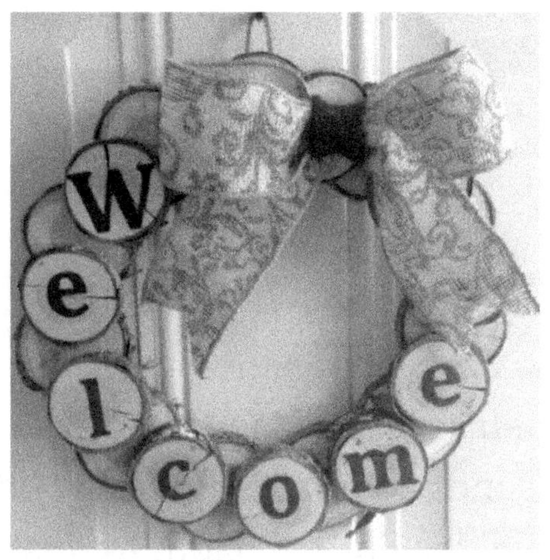

Frames for Pictures

Are you tired of seeing plain wooden frames around your pictures? Yes? Try this out! It is a brilliant design that beautifies your frames with lines, dots, shapes, and several other symbols, almost to the point of creating something complex like motifs.

Let's get started!

Supplies needed

- A pyrography pen.
- A pencil
- A ruler.
- An eraser.

- An abrasive.
- Gloss paints (optional)

Steps Involved

1. Since the frames are already in their right shapes, we will start at the sanding stage. Run a finely gritted sandpaper along the wood grains and then use a dry lint-free cloth to dust off the wood dustings.
2. For frames, you could try out a bit of creativity by either creating something beautiful on your computer and then have them transferred to your wood, or do the designs directly on your wood.
3. You can start your designs by dotting some portions of the wood completely, drawing diagonal lines across another portion of the wood, and then end by drawing treble clefs or bass clefs along the bottoms. You can use your ruler for the lines so that you eventually come out with neat and straight lines. You can also decide to do something simple, like drawing lines diagonally throughout the frame's length.

Another simple design can involve you just decorating the whole length with dots and circles.

4. When you are designing, run the blade of your pyrography pen lightly across the lines you have drawn to burn them. You can make them all thick if you want, but then do that after doing the light lines.

5. When you are done burning, run sandpaper across the burns' surfaces to make the raised grains leveled with the stable surface.

6. To bring out the beauty of your project, you can use a painter's large and rectangular shaped brush to coat the sides of the wood with gloss paint. You could also use a much smaller brush to make slight dustings of gloss across the newly burned designs. You could also make gradual blends of colors; for example, you can paint the circles at the top a very dark red. Then, as you go down to the other circles, you could add a bit of white to lighten it up.

7. You can seal your work with a thin coat of paste wax to give it the needed sheen.

8. Leave the sealant to dry for hours or a whole day, if needed. If you are still not satisfied with the

sheen after it dries, you can apply another thin
layer to it. Wait for that additional layer to dry up
too.

9. Rub the paste wax surfaces with a soft cloth to get
rid of any cloudy impression it may have.

10. Hang your newly decorated frames proudly in
your house.

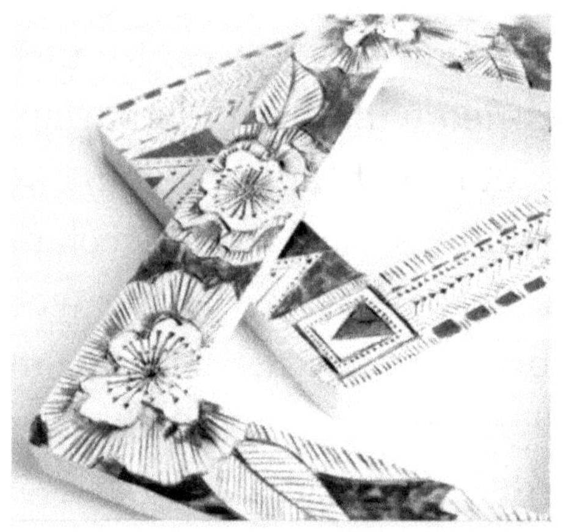

Cutleries

Surely, you'd have wooden cutleries like spoons, forks,
and food rakes in your kitchen. Do you know that with
your pyrography heat tool, you can easily get them
looking even better than ever before? No? Try it out
first, and then make your lovely comments after.

Supplies needed

- Wooden cutleries
- A pyrography heating tool.
- A pencil.
- An eraser.
- Sandpaper of fine grit.

Steps Involved

1. Run a finely gritted sandpaper along the direction the grains of the wood tend towards and then, use a dry lint-free cloth to dust off the tiny wood shavings.
2. Use a sharply tipped pencil to outline your designs on the wood. It could be a small design of the sun peeking out of the clouds. You could even outline tall palm trees all through the length of the spoon.
3. If you cannot handle free-hand sketching, get a design that fits into the wooden cutlery. Instead of using graphite paper, you can just shade the paper's back darkly and trace the outline against the wood.

4. Use a white eraser to clean off the dark marks and other lines that are not needed from the wood's surface.

5. Plug in the heating tool to the socket and then run the tip across the outlines' length once the blade gets hot enough. You can start lightly first and continue with thicker shades later on. It depends on how prominent you want the outlines to be.

6. Run sandpaper across the surface of your burns to make the surfaces smooth and regular.

7. Wipe off the shavings with a lint-free cloth.

8. If you are going to seal this project, use wood-friendly finishes like linseed oil. You are done!

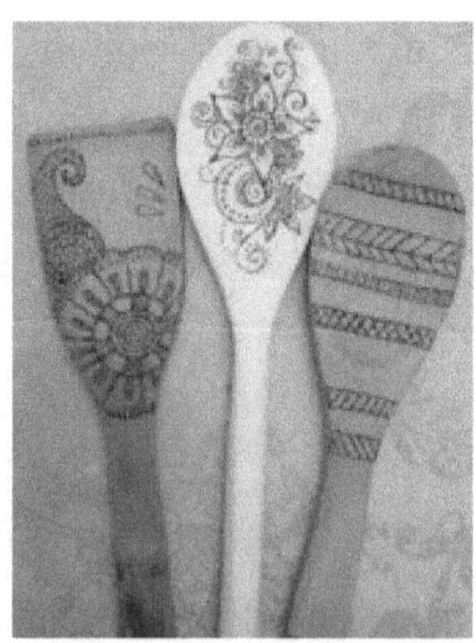

Lion

It's time to do something even deeper! You could fix this project when it's completed to the door of your room to scare off people when you don't want an intrusion. Now, let's do something so real that everyone hears the lion roar angrily at them.

Supplies needed

- A woodburning pen of variable heat.
- Maple wood.
- Versa tool.
- Graphite or carbon paper.
- Sandpaper.
- Design to wood-burn.
- Measuring tape.
- Clear tape.
- Knife blade.
- Transfer tip.

Steps Involved

1. Sand the surface of the maple wood with sandpaper of about 220-grits. Doing this will prevent obstructions when you use your pyrography pen. It will also help the grains of the wood to fade to nothing.

2. You should also use sandpaper to smoothen the edges. Run the abrasive along with the graining of the wood to prevent the wood from chipping.

3. Now, to transfer the design outline to the wood, you'll need to use the tracing method. Make sure you measure the length and breadth of the wood surface you will be working on so that you can know if the design will fit in. It's fine if you want to draw the design with your free-hand, though, but that will require a great skill.

4. Attach the graphic outline of your design to the graphite paper with tape and make sure that it's the dark side that faces the board.

5. Now, use your transfer tip to trace the outlines of your design.

6. When you are done, remove the sheets from the surface and check for any detail you may have missed. If there is any of that sort, you can place the sheets back on the surface and trace them

back. Mind you; you are only tracing the important outlines. Shades and shadows are not to be affected in this step.

7. Once you are sure all the lines have been drawn on the wood surface, erase the ones that are not needed with a white eraser.

8. Now, it is time to burn. This particular step will require you to exercise as much patience as you can. In the lion's outline, you will see several intricate parts like the mane, the eyes, the ears, the snout, and several other features. First, to avoid messes, start burning thinly by using heating devices thin tips. You should also reduce the heat of the pen to get better results with the thin burns.

9. Burn the inner details first before moving on to other thicker lines. To get thicker lines, press the tip to the surface for a longer time.

10. When you are done burning, switch over to your shading tool. This tool will be very useful for parts like the eyeball and the mane. All you need to do is shade so that there's a balance between the dark and the light spots.

11. You may also need to shade the sides of the lines you used to outline the mane.

12. To make deeper illustrations, you can use the knife blade to make grooves and sharp edges. This is one step you should try out for the eyebrows and the mane, especially if you are good at carving wood.

13. To add life to your project, you can add color to it. For this, you can use watercolor pencils. For the eyes, go for something red or nude. For the mane, you can use a color in the junction of red and brown. To create a glossy effect, run a soft brush that has been previously soaked in alcohol across the colorings.

14. Allow the color to dry before running a very finely gritted sandpaper through it to get a smooth surface.

15. Lastly, you have to seal your project. You can use the high gloss form of polyurethane to do that. It gives your project a glossy shine that will keep people staring for ages.

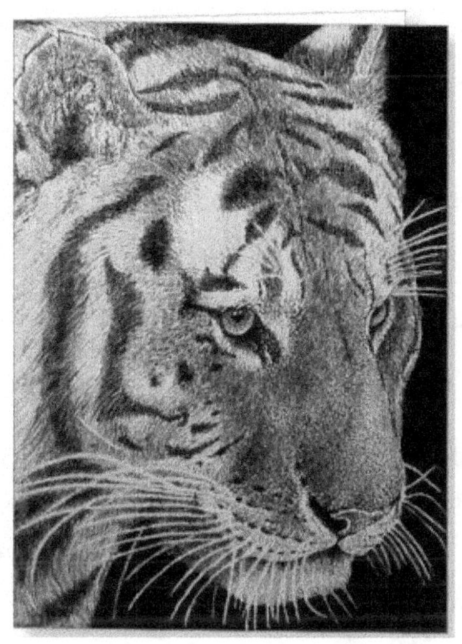

Decorations on a Wooden Vase

Vases hold beautiful things together—flowers. So, your vases must be beautiful too.

Supplies needed

- A pyrography heating pen.
- A pencil.
- An eraser.
- A Wooden vase made of a woodburning material e.g. Beechwood.

- Sandpaper.
- Graphite paper.
- Tape.
- Transfer tip.

Steps Involved

1. Sand the surface of the beechwood with sandpaper of about 220-grits. Doing this will prevent obstructions when you use your pyrography pen. It will also help to reduce the prominence of the wood grains.
2. You should also use sandpaper to smoothen the edges. Run the abrasive along with the graining of the wood to prevent the wood from chipping.
3. Use a lint-free cloth to clean off the sand dust.
4. Draw out your designs on the surface of the wood. You can also use graphite paper to transfer the designs to the surface. Make sure that while tracing, the dark side of the graphite paper is the side that is pinned to the board. You can use designs like the outline of the sun, moon, clouds, villages, trees, flowers, grasses, or anything else that matches your ambiance.

5. When you are done tracing, use a white eraser to clean the unnecessary details.

6. Immediately after that, start burning through the outlines by using a pyrography pen. Start thinly at first before moving on to make dark burns.

7. When you are done burning, switch over to the shading tool to make your project work look even more realistic and beautiful. Apply shadows, dark color hues, and shade the outer edges of your designs. If you are working on the sun's outline, make sure the light part harmonizes nicely with the dark part of the shades.

8. When you are done shading, use sandpaper to smoothen the surface of your wood burn project.

9. You can use polyurethane as a sealant. It will give you this ceramic kind of glossiness that will further ornate your vase. Your vase is ready!

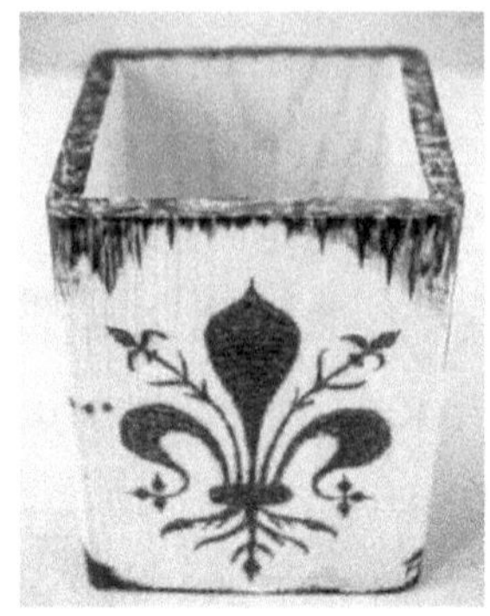

Inscribing Your Name on Wood

Supplies needed

- Pine wood or Maple wood.
- A pyrography pen.
- Lettering fonts.
- Knife blade.
- Sandpaper.
- Graphite paper.
- Eraser
- Versa Tool.
- Transfer tip.

Steps Involved

1. Wrap a square fold of sandpaper around a square box, preferably one with 220-grits.
2. Run it across the surface of your Pine board to level the surface.
3. Sprinkle a little water on the surface in preparation for the next sanding phase.
4. Leave the wooden board to dry for a few minutes.
5. Run another sandpaper across the surface, preferably one of 150-grits.
6. When you are done sanding the surface, use a lint-free cloth to wipe off the dust from the surface.
7. Fix the design of the lettering fonts to a carbon paper with your tape.
8. Make sure that it's the dark side of the graphite paper that faces the board.
9. Tape the sheets of paper to the board.

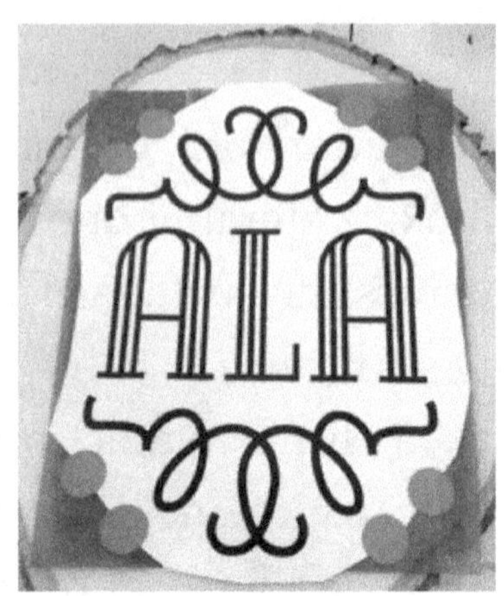

10.Run your transfer tip across the design firmly
   so that you will eventually see the prints on
   the wooden surface.

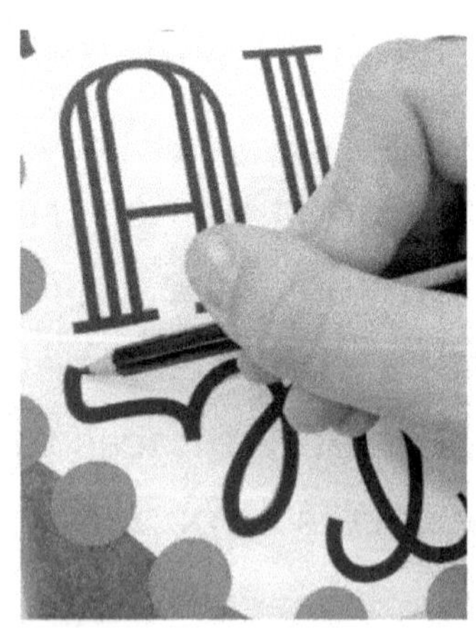

11. Peel the sheets away from the surface of the
    board.

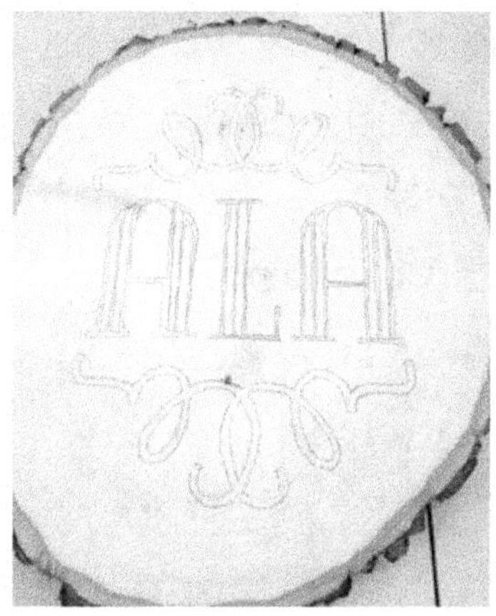

12. Ensure that the tape binding the two sheets
    doesn't get removed in the process because
    you may have missed some outlines.
13. If you did not miss any, you can pick up your
    Pyrography pen.
14. Plug the heating tool into a socket with
    reliable power.
15. Wait for about five-six minutes for the tip of
    the device to become hot.
16. Place the tips at the surface of the wood,
    exactly where the lack outlines are and then,
    burn through it.

17. Do not spend too much time at a spot to prevent dark burns. Start lightly at first.

18. After light burns, you can move on to darken the other outlines of the font.

19. To shade some areas of the design, you can use your Versa tool.

20. When you are done shading, use a white eraser to clean off any lines that weren't needed.

21. You can run a sandpaper across the surface again to smoothen rough edges and surfaces.

22. To add more effect to your work, use the Knife blade to carve out the outlines of the letters out of the normal surface. Run the blade in diagonal directions to hit properly at the wood.

23. Run the sandpaper across the surface again and you are done!

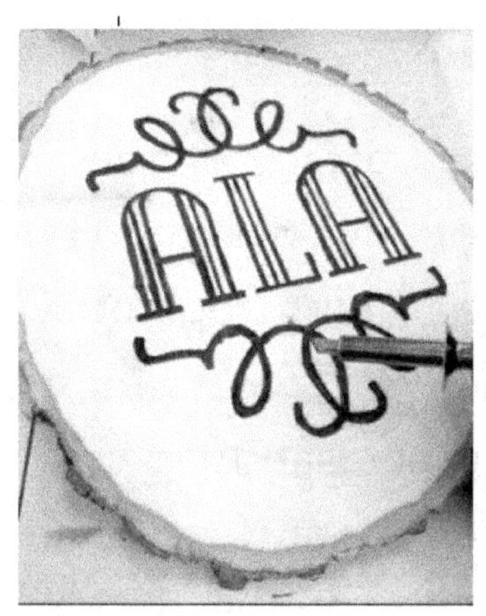

Designing Your Keepsake Treasure Box

Supplies needed

- A box made of a woodburning material e.g. Pine or Maple.
- A Versa tool.
- A pyrography pen.
- Graphite paper.
- Sandpaper.
- Tape.
- A ballpoint pen
- Polyurethane (optional)

Steps Involved

1. Sand the surface of the side of the box that you want your design to be on.
2. Sprinkle a few drops of water on the surface until the wood feels a bit moist.
3. Use another sandpaper, one of finer grit, to smoothen the surface when it dries.
4. Get a copy of the design you want to use. Ensure that it is in a clear black and white format. It could be the design of a flower, the sun or any other creative thing.
5. Attach a sheet of graphite paper to the back and then use a tape to fasten the sheets together.
6. Use another tape to pin the sheets to the wooden surface.
7. Run the tip of your ballpoint pen across the outlines of the design.
8. Remove the sheets from the wooden board after tracing the outlines.

9. Use your heating tool to burn through the wood lightly. Do not leave the blade on a spot for too long.

10. To shade dark areas or to add dark contours and shadows, use your Versa tool. Just move it about the surface of such area like you would move a pencil when shading with it.

11. When you are done, you can use a sandpaper to smoothen the surface.

12. To make your design radiant, you can choose to seal it with a finish like polyurethane. The gaseous sprays are better. Just direct the mouth of the spray lightly across the wood.

13. Your design is done!

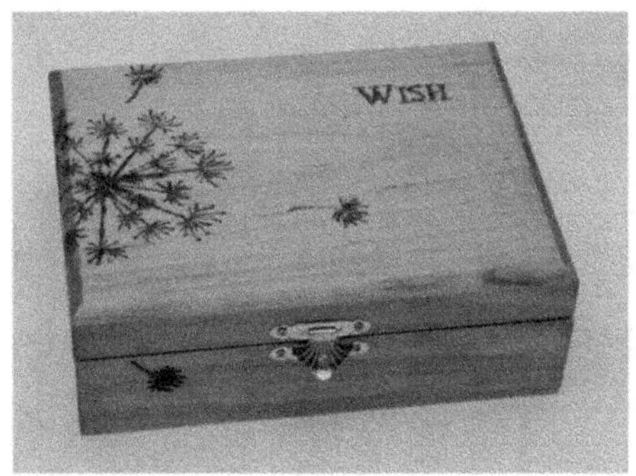

Drawing Nature-Designs

Supplies Needed

- Beechwood.
- A heating tool.
- Graphite paper.
- A ballpoint pen.
- Tape.
- Eraser.
- Sandpaper.
- Versa tool.
- Paste wax.

Steps Involved

1. Cut the beechwood into the shape you want.
2. Run the sandpaper across the wood to smoothen the surface. Make sure you follow the direction the grains in the wood tend to.
3. To smoothen the edges, run the sandpaper out of the board instead of doing it across it.

This will help to prevent the wood from splitting along the edges.

4. After sanding, dust the surface with a lint-free cloth.

5. Since you are working with natural designs, you have to work with the pictures of the sun, trees, leaves, clouds and other related things. Most will require your creativity, while the outline of others can be done with a graphite paper and an actual design.

6. For the outlines of trees, you can get a real design. Tape it to a graphite paper and if you don't have one, you can use colored chalk to paint the back of the design.

7. Tape the sheets to a board.

8. Run the tip of your ballpoint pen across the outlines.

9. When you are done tracing the outlines, remove the sheets from the board.

10. You can start burning the details once you are done tracing.

11. Start burning the outlines lightly at first.

12. For the other details like the ones for clouds, you may have to add a bit of creativity.

13. Pick up a pencil with a sharpened tip and draw wavy outlines on the surface of your wood to represent the clouds. To aid you, you can look at an actual design. The issue here is that tracing the outlines of clouds may not give the same natural vibes as your creativity can.

14. Erase the unneeded lines.

15. Burn through these lines, too, with your heating tool.

16. When you are done, you can decide to either add color or shade.

17. To shade, use your Versa tool. Shade the areas where you think shadows ought to be in and the region of the clouds that mark each curve of cloud.

18. To paint, you can use watercolor pencils. Use it to shade every outline. Make the leaves green, the sun yellow, the soil, a dark brown and the skies a pale blue.

19. To blend the colors nicely, get a soft brush, dip the tips in alcohol and brush it through the outlines. Then, use the padding of your fingers to rub the colors into each other.

20. To create the impression of grasses, you can run your fingers in circles and twirls.

21. When you are done, leave the board to dry.

22. For a more natural look, coat the surface with paste wax. When you see it getting cloudy, use a soft cloth to rub across the surface. That way, your work can have a brilliant sparkle attached to it.

23. Leave your work to dry for as long as a day or two.

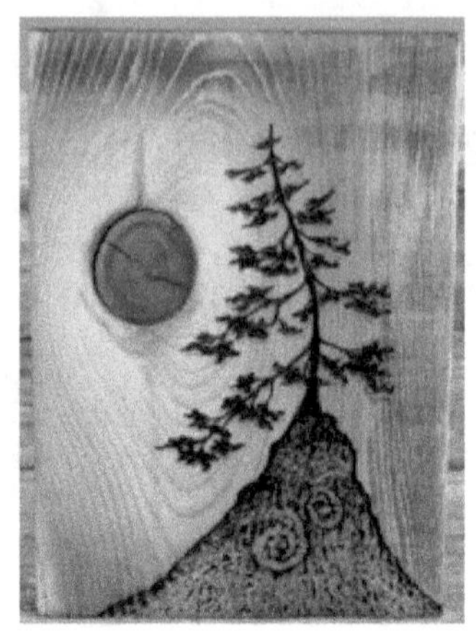

Briar Rose Design

Supplies needed

- A wooden plaque.
- Versa tool.
- Graphite paper.
- Sandpaper.
- A woodburning tool.
- A ballpoint pen.
- Tape.

Step Involved

1. Smoothen the surface of your wooden plaque to get the wood grains out of sight.
2. Sprinkle a few drops of water across the surface to make the wood a bit moist to touch.
3. Smoothen the surface again with a sandpaper of finer grit. This second sanding will ease the tip of your pen when you are burning through the wood.
4. Get a clearly detailed image of a flower to use for your design, probably one in a black and white format.
5. Attach a graphite sheet to the back of the design with a tape.
6. Fix the dark part of the graphite paper to the board a tape.
7. Use a ballpoint pen to trace out the outlines of the flower.
8. Remove the sheets from the wooden board.

9. Insert the plug of your heating tool into a socket and wait for a few minutes for the blade to get hot.

10. Run the heated tip of your pen through the outlines of your flower lightly.

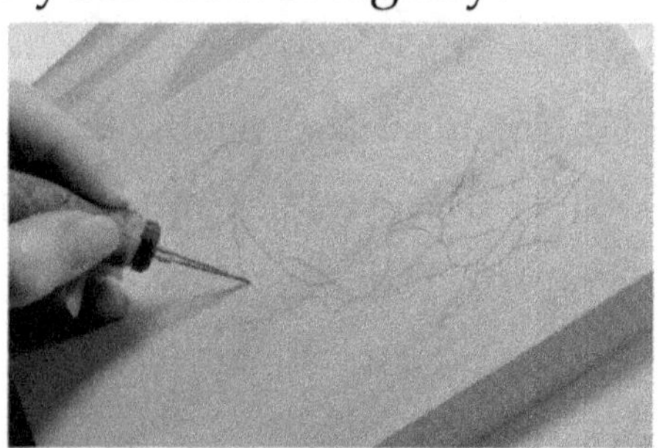

11. Make sure your first burns are as light as possible. Don't grip the handle too tightly.

12. Apply more pressure to the board to get thicker burns. You can use this for the outlines of the flower.

13. To shade the design, run a Versa tool across the surface of the wood.

14. A briar flower is a flower with prickly stems. To create this particular effect on your project, your Versa tool will really come in handy. Lightly run the tip of the Versa tool's blade

diagonally along the stem. Then, shade the sides of the diagonal lines

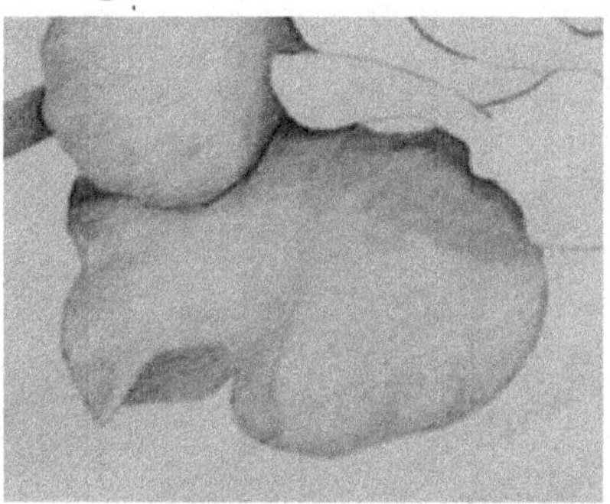

15. To seal your work, use a polyurethane finish.

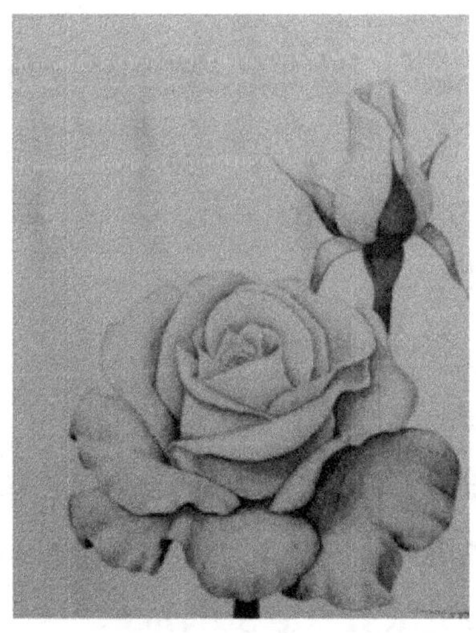

Wooden Advertisement Brand Plaques

Supplies needed

- Pinewood.
- Woodburning pen.
- Versa tool.
- Sandpaper.
- Ballpoint pen.
- Graphite Paper.
- Carbon paper.

Steps Involved

1. Wrap a roll of sandpaper around a wooden box and run it across the surface to smoothen the grains and shallow dents.
2. Sprinkle a few drops of water across the surface to prepare it for the second sanding process.
3. Let the wooden plaque dry for a few minutes.
4. Use another sandpaper of probably finer grit to smoothen the surface.
5. Get the outline of the design you will be making use of. You will need designs of fonts,

the logo of the brand and a few other things you might want to add to the design.

6. Fix the outline of your design to a sheet of carbon paper with a tape.
7. Fix the sheets to the wooden surface with another tape.
8. Use a ballpoint pen to transfer the outline of the design to the wooden surface.
9. You may have to repeat the process above to outline the letters and other things you may want to add to the project.
10. When you are done tracing, peel off the sheet and begin to burn through the lines.
11. Start lightly at first before proceeding to make deeper burns.
12. Use your Versa tool to shade the areas that need to appear as black.
13. When you are done, smoothen the surface with a sandpaper of finer grit to prepare for the finishing.
14. Since most advertisement plaques are placed outside where the sun shines, you might have

to add a finish with an ultraviolet inhibitor. It will prevent the wood from getting oxidized and, in turn, turning to a darker color.

15. You are done!

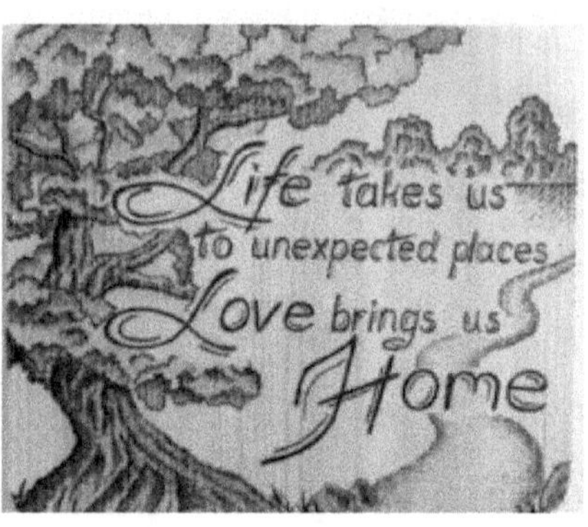

Chapter 5

Fixing Common Woodburning Problems

After making that costly mistake on something very expensive, what do you do? Here, we will go through a list of possible mistakes you can make in your woodburning projects and how you can solve them.

1. Dark burns

This mistake could occur when you leave the tip of your wood burn heating tool for a long time on the wood's surface. To solve this issue, you can use a sanding pen. Sanding pens are tools used in scratching off faded paints from automobiles. However, when using this tool, make sure you do not apply too much pressure on it. It will help to prevent the wood from splitting along the length. For this very reason, use sanding pens for hardwood. If you have something you must correct on a softwood like pine, use sandpaper to correct the error.

2. Wood chipping

This can occur when too much pressure is placed on wood. For example, when you go against the wooden plaque grain when sanding, there could be some break lines along the wood surfaces.

You can use colored filters that go with the wood's tone to hide the chippings to solve this issue. You can also follow the following steps to fix split wood.

- Introduce glue to the split woods.
- Fasten the two ends together with a clamping tool. This will hasten the joining of the two parts.
- Wait until the glue dries before you remove the clamp.
- Use an abrasive to peel off the excess glue.

3. Air bubbles in a finish

This issue could occur if the wood surface were not sealed properly. If it is not dealt with on time, dirt and oils can easily destroy your project. Apart from that, air bubbles make the surface of the sealing rough to touch.

To get rid of the bubbles, use 220-grit sandpaper.

4. Issue of dents on the wood surface

This issue can occur as a result of your rough-handling of the wood. How can you fix this issue? If the dent occurs along the softwood surface, sprinkle a little bit of water on that area. Once this is done, the dent will rise to a level with the regular surface. In case it goes beyond the regular surface, wait for it to dry and then run an abrasive across the surface.

For hardwood, press a moist cloth to the dent and then use a hot iron to press the cloth down on it. This procedure will cause the dent to rise and level up with a stable surface.

The end… almost!

Hey! We've made it to the final chapter of this book, and I hope you've enjoyed it so far.

If you have not done so yet, I would be incredibly thankful if you could take just a minute to leave a quick review on Amazon

Reviews are not easy to come by, and as an independent author with a little marketing budget, I rely on you, my readers, to leave a short review on Amazon.

Even if it is just a sentence or two!

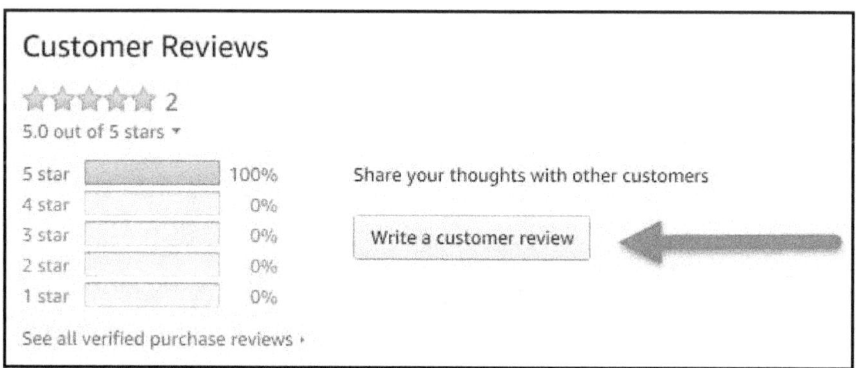

So if you really enjoyed this book, please...

\>\> Click here to leave a brief review on Amazon.

I truly appreciate your effort to leave your review, as it truly makes a huge difference.

Chapter 6

Woodburning Frequently Asked Questions

Is there a contrast between wood-burning and pyrography?

Yes, indeed, there is. Pyrography is an artwork that generally means writing with fire. And the writing can be done on surfaces like rubber, leather, wood, ceramics, anything! Wood burning, however, is only done on wood. Besides, it is a branch of pyrography, so of course, they can't mean the same thing.

What are the uses of the different wood burning tips available?

The universal tip (i.e., the one that works for several functions) is used to burn through the pencil lines or tracings of your design. It is also used to burn straight lines on wood.

The calligraphy tip is good for burning grooves and curves into the wood. It can also be used to write stylishly on wood.

The extra-fine tip is used for burning through outlines that need a higher level of meticulousness like circles, curves, and grooves. It can also be used to burn through very thin lines.

The looped tip is used for shading across the outlines of your designs.

What is the most suitable wood for wood burning?

The best woods for burning are mostly softwoods. Besides that, a good wood should be receptive to stains, easy to burn, soft, should have a low resin or sap content, and minimal grains, and it should be well dried. Examples of wood that fit into this category are Pine and Aspen.

What type of wood should you not use your heating tool on?

1. Do not burn through woods with high resin or sap content.
2. Do not burn on dark woods.
3. Do not burn on woods with rough surfaces.
4. Do not burn on synthetic wood
5. Do not burn on reclaimed wood.
6. Do not burn on wood with high moisture content.

7. Do not burn on wood with prominent grains.

Is it necessary to sand the wood before burning it?

Burning on its own will help you get rid of the parts of the wood surface, contributing to roughness. The only time you may have to sand before burning is when there are uneven patches and gully-like grooves in the wood. You can use sandpaper of 150-grits or something more than that to smoothen the surface.

Is plywood a receptive surface for pyrography?

Plywood is a good surface for wood-burning projects. However, if you burn so deep through the outlines that you reach the glue, it could worsen your health as dangerous fumes will be released.

Can normal pictures be transferred to wood?

Yes, they can. All you need to do is get the picture from your computer's gallery or the internet. From there, print it out on a dry-ink printer like LaserJet. However, at the back of the picture, make sure to attach a graphite paper. You can also color with lead or chalk powder. To transfer totally to the wood, run a pen through the outline of your design.

What way will most easily help me to transfer an image to the surface of my wood?

I guess that will be chalk design. You can get any colored chalk, run it quickly across the back of your design sheets, and then paste it to the surface of your wooden plaque.

What items should be in my tool kit?

In your wood-burning kit, you should have the following items.

1. The wood-burning pen.
2. Several tips for the heating pen.
3. A stand for your pyrography pen.
4. Stamps
5. Stencils
6. Sandpaper
7. Carbon paper
8. Designs

Does the wood have to be sealed after burning?

Sealants are necessary because the procedure before it in wood-burning usually causes the wooden fibers to be pushed to the surface, thereby causing so many irregularities. These irregularities must vanish for the sealant to function.

Can you paint over wood burning?

Well, yes, you can. This procedure is one of the ending processes in wood burning. You can use water-based colors, watercolor pencils, wood gel stains, wax-based pencils, wax-based crayons, latex paints, gel paints, acrylic, pastel paint pens, and so on. Latex paint is excellent on wood. Color pencils are very controllable and can be made to blend easily, harmonize, and unify with the other colors. Acrylic, too, is good. The only downside to using it is that you might need a lot of wood prepping before you can use it.

How easy is it to burn Basswood?

Even though it falls into the category of hardwood, Basswood is very easy to burn. You may have to turn the heat of your heating pen to the highest, but then, it's still easy to make those burns since it is virtually the softest hardwood out there.

How can you test for the dryness of wood before burning designs on it?

You can get a scrap of that same wood, break it open by the middle and then, run your fingers across the fibers. Does it feel moist to touch? If yes, then it is certainly not dry, and so you shouldn't use it to burn your designs. To make it suitable, put it in an electric kiln where it can dry properly.

Why do I have to use lint-free cloths to clean my freshly sanded wooden surfaces?

Lint-free cloths have very thin microfibers that do not just remove the dirt that lies on the surface of the wood. It goes deeper to remove even the ones caught in between the wood fibers! Ordinary cotton cloths won't do this for you

How do I change the tip of my wood burning tool?

The tips have inner threading that allows you to insert it in like you would do a screw. To use another tip, remove the one that was there previously with pliers. But then, before you do this, ensure that the device has been powered off and is cool already. To avoid a situation where the tip fuses stubbornly with the tool, use graphite powder.

How can you clean the tips of your heating tool?

If the device is not hot at that moment, you can use a soft cloth to clean the tip. However, if it is hot, you might have to use sandpaper to scratch the dirt off the tip. Tea strainers too work best to handle this issue.

Do I get a plain or end-grain wood?

Whether the grains on wood are plain or end-grained depends on how it is cut down from the parent tree. A wood plaque with a plain grain is cut down from the growth rings of old trees. Plain grains tend in a direction that is vertical to the normal line of growth of the tree rings. A wood plaque with end-grains were cut from the parent tree with the saw traveling horizontally. With this method of cutting, the wood plaque will emerge with a heart shape that projects towards the back of the wood.

Wood plaques with these central heart shapes usually have a high sap or resin content unlike the ones with plain grains. So, plain grain woods are preferable to the end-grain ones because of their light color tones, light grains, fine surfaces, etc. Your pen's smooth glide will also get less disrupted when burning wood.

Conclusion

Pyrography is a very interesting art that only gets better when it focuses solely on wood. Now, with all the lessons you picked up from this book, you should be able to know the dos and don'ts. One characteristic you must have as a pyrography artist is a patience and steadiness. Not only talent shows in your project, and that's something most crafters don't know.

Your project is a gross collection of every virtue you exercised while working, your emotions, and all of that. So, focus on mixing all those different things in the right proportions to get something mind-blowing and beautiful.

Happy pyrography, artists!